D0008094

Goddess of the Last Minute

LAUGHTER AND LESSONS FROM
AN UNCOMMON QUILTER

ROBBI JOY EKLOW

Voyageur Press

To find out more about our books, visit us online at www.voyageurpress.com.

ISBN-13: 978-0-7603-3429-4

Editor: Margret Aldrich
Designer: Sara Holle
Jacket Designer: Elly Rochester
On the cover: "Fantasy Flowers" quilt © Robbi Joy Eklow

Printed in the United States of America

Library of Congress Cataloging-in-Publication Data

Eklow, Robbi Joy.
  Goddess of the last minute: laughter and lessons from an uncommon quilter / Robbi Joy Eklow.
    p. cm.
  ISBN 978-0-7603-3429-4 (hb w/ jkt)
  1. Quilting. 2. Quilting—Humor. 3. Quilting—Miscellanea. 4. Eklow, Robbi Joy. I. Title.
  TT835.E462 2009
  746.46'041—dc22
                                                    2008033156

For Eileen

Who raised two fine sons, was
a great mother-in-law, and
would have loved knowing
I wrote this book.

Contents

Preface

Are you a Goddess of the Last Minute? I think there are a lot of us out there, scrambling to meet quilt-show deadlines, hurriedly finishing up a quilt to give as a gift, running to the quilt shop or post office just before the doors lock. There may be a little Goddess in all of us.

If you picked this book up because of the title *Goddess of the Last Minute*, you might be under the impression that the material contained within deals with getting things done in an efficient fashion. This is not the case. As all quilters know, efficiency is an elusive thing: seams sometimes need to be resewn, a quilt you want to photograph refuses to hang just right, and you always end up spending twice as long in the quilt shop as you intended. (And twice as much money. If you enter the quilt shop with the intention of purchasing one spool of thread, undoubtedly you will leave with five yards of fabric, one new book, and three sheets of template plastic. All on sale, of course.) My husband, in my defense, will tell you that I am pretty efficient, but only because I'm lazy and would rather spend an hour thinking about the best way to get something done than getting out of my chair and spending twenty minutes to do it in the first place. So, I don't have much to share with you about efficiency—at least not a whole book's worth.

Perhaps you thought this book would help you become more punctual. Pretty much anyone who has had to wait for me knows that I have nothing useful to share on that subject, except maybe that if I really have to be somewhere on time, I write the appointment down as fifteen minutes earlier, so that when I'm running in and apologizing, I'm actually on time.

I also want to make it clear that this book does not contain recipes that you can use to make dinner in fifteen minutes or less. There are no recipes at all in this book, since I do not cook that well or have the slightest desire to improve myself in that department. I don't cook, I don't clean—I make quilts. Art quilts. The kind that have no useful purpose except to beautifully cover a blank spot on the wall. Well, I don't normally hang quilts on my own walls . . . most of them are made for quilt shows that are attended by lots of people who want to look at quilts so they have an excuse to avoid housework and buy quilt fabric. We try to hang quilts on the walls of our house, but I'm always taking them down and shipping them to some quilt show. The one quilt that is always on the wall is in my bathroom. It covers the place where a neighbor kid squirted a cleaning product that contained bleach onto a quilt already hanging there, and onto the wall behind it. The new quilt hides the white spots that showed up on the sponge-painted wall.

The majority of my quilts are made just for the joy of it. I design the quilts on my computer, dye my own fabric, use fusible appliqué, and free-motion quilt them heavily. My quilts get submitted to large quilt shows around the country, and every once in a while I win a ribbon.

The attention given to my quilts has allowed me to pursue a teaching career, sharing my techniques with other quilters around the United States, New Zealand, and even Australia. Traveling so much to teach has taught me that, wherever I go, there are other quilters who have embraced their love of fiber and abandoned all hope of a life without it.

I write a column for *Quilting Arts Magazine* under the byline "Goddess of the Last Minute." It's not a how-to-make-a-quilt column; it's about living life as a quilter. When I was in first grade, I used to read Erma Bombeck in the *Chicago Sun Times*, and I like to think of my column as having a touch of Erma if she would have discovered quilting.

This book is a collection of new essays about the quilting life. In the stories ahead, you'll read about my adventures as an art quilter, mother of two, and traveling instructor; what inspired me to get my first tattoo; how to convince your husband to buy you a sewing machine instead of diamond earrings; how to determine if you have a color obsession; and a few practical quilting tips I've learned along the way.

Thanks for purchasing *Goddess of the Last Minute*, or lugging it home from the library, and thanks for reading. I bet if you quilt you'll see a bit of yourself in these pages and laugh, or maybe you'll see that you are completely different . . . and be relieved.

Acknowledgments

Thanks to:
Brian, as always, who takes really good care of me.

Josh and Sam: Without them, I'd have no reason to write and not much to say. And of whom I am very, very proud.

My mother, who nurtured my love of writing.

My grandmother, who nurtured my love of handwork.

All of my quilting friends: Those I've met in person and those I've only met on the 'net.

All of you who read my stuff and tell me it's funny, and that I should write a book.

Margret Aldrich, who made this book possible.

CHAPTER ONE

Meet the Goddess

My Autobiography in 3,000 Words or Less

It is clear to me now that my addiction to all things fiber happened very early. I blame my grandmother, whom I lived with for a while in Evanston, Illinois, when my mother was first divorced. I was in kindergarten. Grama knitted constantly, and I was the only grandchild, so I was on the receiving end of most of her projects. We had a very symbiotic relationship regarding knitting, although she couldn't teach me to knit, as I was left-handed. We'd pick a project—that was back in the sixties, so crocheted hippy vests, or really long ski hats, or really big ponchos, or really tiny skating skirts, were very popular—and head to the yarn shop. Goodman Yarns displayed their wares in round containers stacked along one wall. I can still picture it. Today, it's a Starbucks, and I still drive by there wistfully, wishing that they hadn't wasted a perfectly good knitting store to sell coffee.

Grama would knit or crochet the object of my desire, and then I'd critique it. The ski hat was great, but the longer it was, the cooler it was, so she'd start a new one that was meant to touch the ground. My doll got a new outfit out of the leftovers. I'm sure that Grama enjoyed seeing me wear her stuff with such glee. Isn't that part of what being a grandmother is all about?

In those times, divorce wasn't common, and living with my grandparents was probably what saved me from having a weird childhood.

My mother didn't knit, sew, or do handwork of any kind, actually, but she was supportive of my first efforts, until the day that Grama introduced me to her old sewing machine. My mother was *certain* that I would sew through my finger. I never did; still haven't to this day.

When I was in second grade, my mother and I moved to Phoenix, away from Grama and Grampa. I kept sewing, although by hand. My first "outfit" was a hand-sewn vest, which I made by tracing around a jumper top. I didn't know about facings, or even hems, so the whole thing was just three pieces of fabric, sewn together, with raw edges. My mother didn't mind if I wore it in public. I had learned to hand sew by raiding my grandmother's rag bag and making little purse things. One year, Grama sent me a toy sewing machine, but I took it apart to see how it worked and never got it back together in one piece. So I had to hand sew until she gave me the old White in high school.

I started beading in Phoenix; I was in third grade at the time. I still have some of the bird fetishes I bought way back then. In sixth grade, back in Evanston, my friend Lily Fantl and I would take the bus downtown, first to Lily's ballet lesson and then to Tom Thumb Hobbies, to buy tubes of seed beads. We were both short, and we'd lie about our age in order to get on the bus for eleven cents. Tom Thumb is still there, and I don't think they sell coffee.

I used to ride my bike to Vogue Fabrics, on Main Street in Evanston. That's still there too. It hasn't changed much at all. Looking back, those childhood years were not what I would call stable. I wasn't abused, and we weren't poor. But my mother didn't think that continuity was important, so she'd move from apartment to apartment, and I changed schools often. In fact, until I got to high school, I never completed two years in a row at the same school. It seemed like I was always the new kid, and I never fit in very well at first. But I talked a lot and made friends quickly, so eventually I'd fit in—then we'd move. Making things with my hands was something that could be a constant in my life.

My mother remarried when I was in seventh grade. We moved again. I kept sewing. I took home economics and "really" learned to sew. Except the teacher never noticed the way I was pinning seams: on the seam line, pin head to pin point. I had to take each pin out as I went along. It took forever to sew a simple seam. I persevered and finished a pair of "rompers," made out of double-knit, with set-in sleeves and a zipper. They even fit.

I sewed a lot of my clothes in high school and started hand embroidering. My stepfather was a sales representative for a company that made chambray work shirts, sweat pants, and sweat jackets. At the time, they were sold in hardware stores, to workman and hunters. He gave me the samples when he was done with them so that I could embellish and wear them. I wore embroidered work shirts with the old poncho my grandmother knit. I also inserted embroidered ribbon into my blue jeans to give them bigger bells, and to make them longer when I wore out the bottom of the pant legs. (That was in the olden days when you had to wear out your denim yourself, and holes in the knees were not a good thing.) I embroidered so much that when I went to summer camp, I set up a class and taught other campers. Everyone got a small hoop and threads. I moved on to painting my jeans and wore a brown pair almost every day. I looked like a misguided refugee from Woodstock.

I saw my first patchwork quilt at Lynne Holdridge's house, probably in 1972. Lynne and I were freshmen in high school, best friends. The quilt was a Grandmother's Flower Garden, made by her father's grandmother and given to Lynne for her room. Mrs. Holdridge also knew how to make window treatments. I remember one year she came to visit, and the two Mrs. Holdridges made the living-room drapes together. I was impressed. Lynne and I sewed together too— Lynne is six feet tall, and I'm just under five feet, so we could make clothes that actually fit us.

When the great Bicentennial quilt revival hit, Lynne made a comforter for her boyfriend. It had half-square triangles in blues and greens and was tied. She got the pattern out of the *Chicago Tribune*. I started a red, white, and blue Drunkard's Path but never finished it. The Drunkard's Path pattern, in case you don't know, is made out of quarter circles, pieced onto a square. It is not for sissies, and the fact that I cut out the pieces by layering them six deep and using an electric scissors did not help. One year, I stored the quilt in my college dorm at Purdue over the summer, and I never saw it again. They claimed to have lost the box. Years and years later, they found the box and asked me if I wanted it back. I was too broke to pay for the shipping, so I let it go. If you see a badly pieced Drunkard's Path running around somewhere in Indiana, it could be mine. Well, someone else would have had to put it together, but if you see red with polka dots, blue with white stars, and probably terribly done stripes, you should ask the owner if they got those quilt pieces from the resale shop.

I majored in Engineering in college; I was the only woman on my dorm floor in that degree program. Most of the women were in Elementary Education or other more traditionally feminine programs. Oddly—very oddly, I thought—I was also the only one who had brought a sewing machine to college.

Brian and I started dating my freshman year, and he quickly learned that I loved to sew. The dorms used to sponsor dances, with formal attire and multiple bands, at the student union. We lived in different dorms, so we went to two sets of dances. I sewed all of my dresses. Brian would go to the thrift store and buy an old tuxedo, and I'd make his suspenders or a cummerbund to go with it. He looked like a waiter, but it was fun. Since Brian is six foot two and I am under five feet, the dancing wasn't that elegant. Dinner was the big event, as well as the dressing up.

When we got married our senior year, Brian bought a pair of left-handed Gingher shears for me. Later, he had them engraved with my name.

I didn't sew my wedding dress, but my bridesmaids sewed theirs. Lynne was living in Texas. Jennifer was with me in Indiana at Purdue. Fran was still in Illinois and pregnant with her first son, so luckily the dresses were made out of Quiana, a stretchy, shiny knit, and they were pretty much just long blouses with raglan sleeves.

Brian did not go to the resale shop for his tuxedo this time; he rented a white one. With long tails. His grooms-men wore powder blue tuxedos with frothy shirts. If you have seen *Dumb and Dumber*, you have seen the tuxedos from my wedding.

The winter after we graduated was very cold, and I began to quilt again. Templates were still being used for the most part, but a mother-daughter team, Helen and Blanche Young, wrote a book about using strips of cardboard to mark strips of fabric with notches, to make Trip Around the World quilts. I started collecting fabrics and, when I was pregnant with Josh, made my first baby quilt from the Youngs' meth-ods. It was pieced from polyester/cotton blends and tied with yarn at the corners of each block. I was going to quilt it, but I was a terrible hand quilter back then—I'm sure my idea to use dental floss to make the quilt stronger didn't help. Josh and my daughter Samantha used that first quilt a lot; I think we still have it, shoved in the back of a closet.

I collected more fabric on Saturday jaunts to quilt shops. My budget was ten dollars a week. At that time, it would go a long way, and I collected a lot of solids. I made a few Amish-style quilts and got better at hand quilting. By then I had the two babies, who were rowdy, so I'd have to sew at night and hand quilt by day. I was worried they'd swallow a needle, so I'd unthread the needle every time I stopped quilting to check on them, feed them, or change diapers. It was slow going.

Our first family vacation was to California, to visit my uncle in Santa Monica and Brian's brother in Santa Clara. The trip was chaotic. The toddlers made a mess of everything—the plane, the rental car—and Josh flushed a box of tampons down Uncle Bill's toilet. I realized that I needed a sanity break, a vacation away from the babies. The next summer, Brian took the kids to Florida to visit his parents while I went to West Virginia to take a week-long quilting class with Nancy Crow, the godmother of art quilting.

The main thing I learned from Nancy was that I needed to have a quilting space of my own. We were in the market for a house and found one—with studio space—in Third Lake, Illinois, which at the time was the northern edge of suburban Chicago.

The studio was a godsend. It gave me a place to work in peace in the evenings, and I could shut the door on the mess.

My kids thought that every mother had a studio; when they made a new friend, they sometimes asked what their mother did in *her* studio. During the day, I hand quilted on an old-fashioned queen-size quilt frame set up in the living room, which had no furniture. Josh and Sam would play in the family room and leave me alone. I could hear them and ignored most of the arguments between them, unless it sounded like they would be drawing blood. I spent a long time on an Ocean Waves quilt, getting the straight lines of black hand quilting done in the main blocks and working on three out of four borders. The quilt still needs one more border and feathered wreaths in the plain blocks. I will probably never complete that quilt; I will leave it for a descendant to discover and delight in finishing. Or not.

I hand quilted every Tuesday night, when I drove closer to the city to join a quilting bee. I never finished any of those projects either, but I made some great friends.

The quilting guild that I belonged to had a challenge one year. Everyone got a packet of sixty-four different fabrics. The challenge was to make a quilt using each one of the fabrics. I made a quilt that had fan shapes in the corner. Samantha was taken with one of the blocks that had a print featuring dolls and kept swiping the block and hiding it in her room. Finally, I promised her she could have the whole quilt, as soon as it was finished, if she'd stop running off with the parts. I had to keep adding beads and embroidery to it, to stall until the deadline of the challenge in order to keep the quilt out of Sam's room. Finally we hung the quilt in her room. When she was mad at me for some offense, she'd carefully snip off one bugle bead and present it to me, as a token of her lack of esteem.

The next year, the guild challenge was a charm quilt, again sixty-four fabrics, but each piece had to be the same shape. That is when I started fusing my quilts. I used a pattern that looked like a Persian design and fused all of the blocks onto a flannel background. I fused the flannel background to a piece of fusible fleece. I fused the backing to the quilt. There was so much fusible, that when I started free-motion quilting, the needle got gunked up every few inches. I was also using the wrong brand of fusible webbing, a product that wasn't meant to be sewn through. However, I wanted the prize—a basket full of fabrics—so I kept at it. I bound the quilt with a knitted fabric, with gold threads running through it. The whole thing was terribly tacky, but I won a bunch of fabric, and my career in fusing was launched. The problem was coming up with some good design ideas.

I can't remember the circumstances, but I found a magazine called *Maison Française*. The cover featured a cobalt blue flower pot, with a lime green plant. I loved the color combination. I loved the pictures in the magazine. *Maison Française* is published in France, in French, so the pesky text doesn't get in the way because I can't read much of it. ("Piano" either means "main" or "first" in regards to the floor of a house, and that's about as far as I can get.) But I can figure out how much things cost when they are shown in euros.

I also found *Brava Casa*, another home dec magazine published in Italy, in Italian of course. Both magazines are very high-style, high-end home design—at least I think so. And the Europeans are a few years ahead of us in color design. I bought issues when I could find them and studied the pictures. I started pulling out pages with vases, teapots, and other vessels that had great shapes and began putting them into quilts. I traced around the edges of the objects and created puzzle quilts with intersecting outlines. I created still-life quilts—no flowers, but lots of vases.

I'd been using my own hand dyes and soon dropped commercial fabrics altogether. I started using more and more free-motion machine quilting. Eventually, I won a few ribbons and started teaching to guilds across the country.

Now I do most of my designs on the computer, using Adobe Illustrator. All of my quilts are done using fused appliqué; no edges are turned. I have an APQS Millennium long-arm to do the quilting, which is all unmarked free motion.

I'm about to move my quilting in a new direction, incorporating paints, maybe even turning edges as in traditional appliqué, and using the computer to make block designs that are circular and will allow others to use my patterns as a base to design their own quilts. I hope you'll pay attention and follow me!

Take My Advice

I was reading the advice column "Dear Abby" and had to laugh at a letter from a woman who recently turned forty. She wanted money for a new sewing machine as her gift. Instead, her husband gave her diamond earrings. There were some other issues: she didn't get along with her husband's family, and he hadn't acted very graciously when he bestowed her with the earrings. They had a fight, and she didn't want the earrings. Now, normally, I think Abby has pretty good advice. But in this case, she suggested an apology from the woman to her husband, and then marriage counseling. She never answered the sewing-machine issue.

I would like to step in and offer a better answer.

Dear "Ticked Off in Rhode Island":
Your husband is indeed a buffoon for not paying attention to your need for a sewing machine. Diamond earrings are certainly not that useful; however, at least he won't ask you to mend his shirts.

He probably didn't think a sewing machine was that romantic. Luckily, you hold the power to solve the problem in your own hands: a credit card.

I myself have dealt with this issue several times.

The first time was in high school, when my uncle—who is not a buffoon but didn't know I wanted a sewing machine—bought me a calculator for my birthday. I'm sure he thought it was a useful gift, as calculators were the latest electronic toy. My solution was to return the calculator and buy a sewing machine, adding on a small amount of my own money to complete the purchase. I am sure that if I mentioned this to my uncle now, he would be delighted that I made that decision, as I did make excellent use out of that machine. I took it to college and made a lot of clothes with it. In the meantime, calculators dropped in price so much that my college calculator was like a small computer.

Later on, when my fifteenth wedding anniversary approached, I wanted a better sewing machine. My husband understood this, having bought me several small pieces of jewelry that I never wore, so he bought me a very nice top-of-the-line sewing machine. Of course, we did have many discussions leading up to the sewing-machine purchase, such as, "Why do we have to spend all that money on that old car you got from your grandfather? You don't drive it." "Why do we have to paint that old car you don't drive?" And finally, "Let's stop in the sewing-machine store and look at stuff on the way home from putting your grandfather's old car in storage."

He did buy me diamond earrings a few years later. They sit in a drawer, and I keep forgetting I even own them until he points it out and wonders why I never wear them.

I will tell you why my husband bought the diamond earrings: He was desperate. My husband, and I'm sure many men like him, look forward to Christmas, major birthdays, and anniversaries the same way I look forward to doing my income taxes. Except that he thinks the IRS is happier with my taxes than I am with his presents.

He thought that every woman would want something expensive to hang off the side of her face. His intentions were good. He's getting better, most of the time. I wasn't that thrilled with my present last Christmas (two pairs of socks, two nightgowns, and some chocolates), but he made it up on Valentine's Day with an iPod.

His next big worry is my fiftieth birthday, which is coming up shortly—in fact, a few days before my tax return is due. I wonder which of us is more stressed?

But this isn't about me, it's about you. Here's what you should do, my dear "Ticked Off in Rhode Island": Return those earrings. Buy a cheaper pair and wear those. Your husband won't know the difference anyway—he probably only bought them because that's how much money he wanted to spend, and if you have long hair, he'll never even see them. On the way home, stop at a sewing machine dealer and buy the nicest machine that you think you can afford. Wrap it up and tell your husband you have bought your own present for whatever holiday is coming up, even if it is St. Patrick's Day. Tell him that from now on, he can buy you accessories for the sewing machine, or fabric, for all of your holidays. He can even take the easy way out and get gift certificates at the local quilt shop and let you continue to do the picking out of the presents. You can even make his life easier by purchasing said items yourself, ahead of time, and telling him what he got you. I did this for many years, "Look honey, you bought a walking foot for me for my birthday! And all this fabric for Mother's Day! You're good until October when I'll go to a quilt show and tell you what you got me for Halloween!

Goddess of the Last Minute

The Goddess of the Last Minute was born one April when I was in Paducah, Kentucky, for the annual American Quilter's Society show. One of the booths set up in a small vendors' mall downtown was offering plastic, engraved nametags for a few dollars. The idea is that you would have your name and your guild put on the tag, and there was a small hole that you could put the post of your guild pin through. I decided to have "Goddess of the Last Minute" engraved on the pin, because I think I'm very good at getting things done at the last minute. I used a Quilt Tack plastic basting device to attach a clock charm to the pin. I liked the irony of the goofiness of the title and the hastily tacked-on clock against the corporateness of the nametag, carefully engraved.

I wore the nametag to my guild meetings, and people started asking me where they could get one of their own, as many of them claimed to also be Goddesses of the Last Minute. I carved a stamp with the title and made Shrink Plastic pins. Sold a *lot* of them for three dollars each at the boutique at my local quilt guild's show.

In 1990, I bought my first Apple computer, a Mac LC. Clarisworks was a software application that came with the computer. The registration form asked for a title. Ms. or Mrs. seemed boring, and knowing that Apple gave people amusing job titles at that point, I filled out the form with my Goddess designation. Of course, Apple sold my name and address, and mail started arriving addressed to Robbi Joy Eklow, Goddess of the Last Minute. Or sometimes the whole "Minute" didn't fit and it would cryptically just say "Goddess of the Last Min."

I loved the junk mail. Two Apple-related magazines came with a trial offer; one addressed me properly with my Goddess title. The other didn't. So of course, when it came time to pick one and pay for a renewal, I chose the former. I had to explain the title to a customer-service rep for the magazine once.

One day when my mother was visiting, I came in from the mailbox laughing at all the junk mail addressed to "her Goddessness." I tried to explain to my mother that it was a joke, but I don't think she got it. I'm sure she thought I was suffering from delusions of grandeur.

I continued to use the title whenever I could and sold the genuine plastic pins whenever I could. When I was invited to write a column for *Quilting Arts Magazine*, I asked them to allow me to use "Goddess of the Last Minute" as my by-line. And it fits, because it seems that they always use whatever column I write immediately before the deadline.

I want to explain about the last minute thing a little bit. It does not mean spending your whole life procrastinating until the very last second. I'm referring to the ability to know how to get things done quickly and efficiently so that I can take advantage of an opportunity quickly if one comes up.

A good example would be one quilt I made, "Sock It to Me." I had a quilt top in progress, on a Monday, and found out about a contest with a deadline of that Friday. I dropped everything—and by everything I mean all housework, cooking, cleaning, errand running, whatever took me away from the sewing machine—and quilted it. I already had film on hand to take slides (that was back in the days before digital cameras). There was a one-hour slide developer about a mile away from my house. I took slides, ran the film over, did the paperwork while I waited for the slides to develop, and then ran over to the post office.

It is *much* easier to finish quilts right before a deadline now that most shows take digital images. I keep a big supply of blank CDs and big envelopes, and in most cases, the entry forms are available on the internet, so I don't have to waste time trying to find them.

Part of the trick is convincing your family to be self-sufficient when you need to meet a deadline. It helps not to lose your patience. I'm not very patient with others who leave things to the last minute and expect me to pick up the pieces for them. Their failure to plan does not make an emergency mine. I also try to leave time in for things to go wrong. In general, I plan to have a quilt done a week before the deadline—although, every once in a while, I come across a new deadline I'd like to try meeting and just go for it. This year, between Christmas and New Year's Eve, I discovered some unencumbered time, finished up a quilt quickly, and submitted it to two quilt shows before the week was over!

Why I Love My Studio

My husband Brian and I lived in a tiny condo in Chicago after college. There was no room for a sewing-machine cabinet, and for some reason I can't remember, we had a flimsy glass dining table. I was afraid to put the sewing machine on that table; it felt like it would wobble the whole thing to pieces. I would sit on the floor and operate the sewing machine control pedal with my knee. Not very comfortable.

We moved into a larger condominium when the kids were babies, with a sturdier dining table. However, Josh was an active toddler, and machine sewing with him around was a risky activity—I was afraid he'd get hurt. I did my piecing at night, after he and Samantha were asleep, or when they took naps. I hand quilted, and I could do that while keeping a close eye on them.

I took a workshop from a very famous quilter and brought the one quilt I had managed to finish for show and tell. She said "You aren't a very dedicated quilter if that is all you managed to do in a whole year." Not the nicest thing to say. I'm sure she had forgotten how hard it was to get anything done while taking care of toddlers. During the workshop, however, I came to see that what I needed was a space of my own.

We had been hunting for a house—in an area with good schools, affordable, all the regular requirements for a first house. I added the need for my own studio to the list, and Brian agreed, as long as I promised not to expect to buy furniture for the room before we had furniture in the rest of the house.

Brian came home from work one day and was practically dancing in the kitchen. This is a man who rarely gets excited about anything, unless he's watching a football game. He had found an empty lot in a new development, way out on the northern edge of the Chicago suburbs. The builder was going to put up a four-bedroom house on the lot, thus allowing for each kid to have their own room and for me to have my studio. Best of all, the house was across the street from a small lake, with a beach and swimming area.

I took over the second-largest bedroom for my studio, my reasoning being that the two smaller ones would be better for each of the kids so that they wouldn't fight over who had the larger room.

A "working wall" or "design wall" is an essential tool when working on large quilts. It can also be used to pin up completed quilts in order to take photographs. One was created by purchasing two sheets of foam insulation, mounting them on the wall with t-pins instead of nails, and then covering them with two pieces of wide, black felt. The join between the felt sheets was simply made by putting in pins. Instead of trimming off the excess felt, it was left drooping and can be draped over a closet door to hide it when taking photos of larger quilts.

Furniture was scrounged from an outlet store in a nearby mall, my favorite piece being a wood trestle dining table. This was covered with two layers of cotton batting and a top layer of black canvas, to become a giant ironing board. Eventually two different sewing machine cabinets were acquired; each has a drop-down leaf that is normally dropped down but can be extended to make even more working space.

Bookcases are used for storage of fabric. A few actual books live in here, but most of them are scattered around the house.

Some tools, like rotary cutting rulers, hang from wire grids bought on clearance at kitchen stores.

The main storage is in my "wall of drawers" (which you can read all about in the essay "All My Life in Drawers").

I like to listen to music or watch TV while working on quilts. One corner holds all the AV equipment: the TV, CD/DVD player, VHS, and stereo tuner. I have extra speakers, bought years ago, but I keep forgetting to install them. Since I like to stay up late and didn't want to keep the kids up all night, I bought a wireless headphone setup. Being in my own little sound bubble helps my concentration, and I've noticed that the kids and my husband don't interrupt me when I'm wearing headphones. If they do come in, I can pretend I don't hear them.

My studio is my favorite room in the house. I can go hide in there when the family is being annoying. I don't have to clean it up unless I feel like it. And all my favorite stuff lives in there, waiting for me to come play.

All My Life in Drawers

Several years ago, I discovered that the plastic drawer storage units available in office supply stores are perfect for storing sewing things. The drawers are shallow—about two inches deep, fourteen inches from front to back, and eleven inches from side to side. They come in sets of six, with casters. The neat thing is that you can remove the lid and not install the casters. This allows you to stack the units on top of each other, as high as you can reach. For me, that is sixteen drawers high. You can also buy units with drawers that are double deep; these too stack, and they mix and match with the shallower drawers.

When I was searching for ways to get all my stuff under control, I realized I love these storage units. They fit perfectly under my worktable, and actually, since you can adjust them, they fit perfectly almost anywhere. I started to collect them whenever they were on sale for half price. I was putting everything I could possibly think of in these drawer units and lining one wall of my studio with them. My husband thought it was odd the day that the office store delivered six of them to our porch at the same time. I keep buying the drawers, reasoning that if we ever move, all the movers have to do is tie the drawers closed and roll my whole studio into the truck. The fact that we have lived here for twenty years and will probably stay put has nothing to do with it.

In the meantime, the drawers—or, as I call them, the "wall o' drawers"—hold a lot of stuff. Thread, templates, paper supplies, pins, notions, and rotary cutters and scissors (in cutlery trays). My son Josh made a short little movie about my wall of drawers. He found it odd that I have a drawer for rotary cutters, and another drawer for rotary cutters, and a third drawer for rotary cutters. And when we looked in the scissor drawer, there were rotary cutters in there too. A friend who has never been to my house saw that video and was worried that I may have a touch of obsessive-compulsive disorder. She thought that my whole house was as organized as my wall o' drawers. I assured her that that is certainly not the case; in fact, the rest of my studio and my house is one big mess. A friend of my son saw the video and asked him where the "junk drawer" is. Josh told him the rest of the house is a junk drawer.

I used to have a great labeling system for my wall o' drawers. I printed out labels naming the contents of the drawers, along with their address. I'll explain the address part. Consider each stack to have a letter, starting with A on the left end, and then each drawer has a number, starting with a "1" on the top. So, a drawer with a label that says "A1" is the leftmost drawer, on the top of that stack. Drawer C3 is two stacks over to the right, three drawers down. This is very handy to know when you have pulled the drawer out of the wall unit to have a better look at the contents.

However, I tend to rearrange the drawers—certainly sharp objects do better in a lower drawer, as do heavier objects. And there was that one time I bought a whole bunch of new, double-deep drawers and managed to rearrange everything so they are on the bottom. Housing my VHS tapes. (One day, I will toss them and fill the space with something else that is heavy.) So, now, I use index cards to create labels. I skip the address and just write the contents in big letters on the cards.

I can usually find everything very quickly if things are in the right drawer. I have my thread collection divided into its own tower, yellow threads being in one drawer, orange in another, metallic thread in the next . . . you get the idea.

I was surprised to have a major crisis a few weeks ago.

I have some embroidery software for my sewing machine. I can design stuff on my computer, bring it into this special software, and then the software will convert it to something that the sewing machine can stitch out. It's pretty nifty. The software is expensive, so to combat piracy, the publisher forces me to use a "dongle" whenever I want to run the software. The dongle plugs into the USB port on my computer and tells the software that, indeed, it is a licensed copy. If I gave someone a copy of the software, they couldn't do a thing without the dongle. The dongle is essentially worth the cost of the software. At least, that is what I think. I could be wrong. I have been before. I don't know for sure, because this software is on loan to me from the manufacturer.

The other day, I found out that the software company wants their stuff back. That means the CDs, the owner's manuals (which I have kept neatly in the box along with the CDs), and the dongle. I needed to find the dongle. I usually keep the dongle in my studio, in the top left drawer, in my "wall o' drawers." The drawer is marked "PC stuff." The dongle is attached to a USB hub, which should make it easier to find. The dongle alone is tiny, only a few inches long. It looks like a clothing tag that should be removed. I could not find it. I looked in the top drawer of my sewing cabinet, another place that would make sense for it to be. No dice. Then I started having a hot flash. (I seem to have hot flashes when I have either had a margarita or am under stress. This was the latter, although a margarita might have been helpful just then.) I checked the drawer where I keep all the spare parts for my sewing machine. The ones that I don't use that much, as opposed to the drawer in the sewing cabinet that holds stuff that gets used all the time. It wasn't in there either.

I thought I found it for a second, because there *was* a dongle in that drawer, still sealed in plastic with a CD that must have come with the machine. I studied it for a while to think whether there was any chance my dongle could have made its way into a sealed bag. I decided this was not possible. On the other hand, I was wondering how the dongle managed to disappear like this after I had spent five years carefully protecting it from loss. Why, I even bought the laptop just to run the software, as it would not play with my preferred computer, a Mac, at the time.

In the process of ransacking my studio, desperately looking for the dongle, I found a bunch of other things I had been missing: several sewing machine feet, the installation disk for my printer, and two USB hubs I didn't even know I owned. That's one nice thing about losing things; I tend to find ten missing objects for every one thing I'm actually looking for. Also, whatever room I'm searching tends to get cleaned up.

I was starting to get nervous though, and the room seemed really hot. I started wondering if I should just tell the software company that I wanted to buy the package, so that I wouldn't have to admit I lost the dongle. Then I emailed them, saying I had the dongle in a very safe place . . . could I have some time to find it? Would they charge me if I had permanently lost it? Why did I even bother borrowing stuff like this when I *know* that I lose things? Why do I have so much clutter? Isn't this house a mess? I'll never find this thing.

The situation was deteriorating. I had looked through the same drawers over and over. PC-stuff drawer, drawer in the sewing cabinet, extra-sewing-machine-stuff drawer, desk drawer, PC-stuff drawer. . . .

I gave up, took a shower, then came back and opened the drawer marked "Computer Input." This drawer holds computer mouses (or is it mice?), old digital cameras, memory sticks (oh look, I just found the memory stick I use to back up my writing . . .), and about twenty rewriteable CDs that have no labels. And the dongle. Problem solved!

And my studio is so much neater. Next, I am going to look for the quilt I lost about three years ago. The last thing I remember is thinking, "I hope I remember that I put this here." It was in a white bag, which frightens me . . . what if it got thrown out in the garbage? I thought I shipped it off for photography with some other quilts, but when I looked on the list of quilts in the box, a question mark was next to this one. So it must be here somewhere. Unless it got thrown out.

I have looked for it occasionally. At least it isn't borrowed, because my biggest fear when someone loans me something is that I'll lose it. Kathleen has lent me some fabric ink. I know exactly where it is. It's in the drawer marked "Misc. Electronic." Excuse me while I go relabel that drawer to read, "Stuff borrowed from Kathleen."

All in all, my drawer system works wonders, except when I can't find anything. I can see a time when everything I own will be encased in "walls of drawers," and all I'll have to do when we move is tape them up and roll them onto a moving truck.

The Right Place to Write

The first thing I have to do when it's time to write something is find the right place to write. It's not as easy as you would think. Given that I use a laptop, any flat surface should do. But that's not true. When I write my Goddess column, it must be done in one fell swoop. I'll think about what I want to write for a few days, searching for a new idea, and then when it comes, it's as if it was stored up in my head somewhere in one package, and if I don't open the chute and let it out all at once, it goes away. I can't write at home with my husband around. If he's near and I laugh at something, he asks what was so funny, and when I turn to tell him, the idea goes into hiding. Sometimes I turn my head away from the computer screen for a moment, to rest my eyes, while the new sentence forms in my head. If one of my kids is sitting on the couch, they'll ask why I am staring at them, and the idea is gone.

So, I have to wait until very late at night, when everyone else is asleep (or in the case of the kids, out with their friends), and then I can write.

One book that I am reading, about writing, suggests that you pick an hour and a half every day and write for those ninety minutes—no matter where you are, no matter what day it is. No vacations. This man either has no family, or they all hate him because he ignores them. Nonetheless, it's a good idea. When I wrote my first quilting book, I tried to work every morning, but I was too distracted at home. The phone would ring, I'd notice clutter, there would be some good cookies in the kitchen, I'd have a quilt idea. Before I knew it, the day would be gone. I decided I'd go to the local pie restaurant and write there. My habit when eating out is to look and see if they have electrical outlets near a comfortable table. I found one there, in a corner that didn't happen to have windows. Every afternoon at one o'clock I went to the pie restaurant. It didn't matter what I did all morning or whether I'd had lunch; at one o'clock, off I'd go and sit at my table. It was right after their lunch rush with a stretch long enough before they got crowded for dinner. And if I managed to keep working long enough until the supper hour, I'd call my husband and tell him to come join me for a meal.

The table was in the back, near the bathroom. Which was a good thing, because the waitstaff knew that I wanted to be left alone except for refills on my soda. After an hour of writing, I'd be running to the bathroom every twenty minutes or so. A secluded table meant I didn't have to grab my laptop each time. Training the wait staff took some time too. In the beginning, they'd ignore the fact that I was wearing headphones and ask me every five minutes if I needed anything. Finally they learned to leave me alone, even to the point of ignoring the puddle of condensation around the soda glass. If I had ordered a meal, I left a generous tip. If I had merely ordered a soda, with numerous refills, I tipped by the hour.

When I was done with the text portion of the book, I needed to work at home, with a larger computer monitor, so I said goodbye to the staff. My afternoon stint was over, but I'd see them in the evenings, with Brian, for dinner or coffee as usual. The manager said she missed me and offered to store the monitor in the back room, if I would bring it in, but I declined.

When I started writing this second book, I thought I'd find a new place to write. But I needed that table with the electrical outlet. And a bathroom nearby. Maybe free internet access, because sometimes I wanted to look something up. (But on the other hand, I'd probably play some internet card game all afternoon, given the chance, so internet access was probably not a good thing.)

Yesterday, I tried the local bookstore, thinking it would be nice to browse through the magazines before writing. That didn't work, mainly because my laptop had a problem and it wouldn't run. It took me two hours to finally decide it wasn't the battery, it was the software. In the meantime, I bought a fancy coffee, a bagel and cream cheese, and a CD about learning to speak Italian.

I would have gone to the pie restaurant, but I didn't get started until three o'clock, and that wasn't going to allow me enough time.

Today, I could call around to interview new spots, but they'd think I was very weird. "Hello, I'm writing a book. I need to find a table near the bathroom, with an electrical outlet. And all I want to order is a soda. With free refills. I'll be there from one to five. Okay with you?"

I think I'll just set up house at the pie restaurant again.

Make It Work

I have always liked to tinker around with things, either fixing something broken, improving something else, refurbishing, or in some cases, breaking something that probably should have been left alone.

The earliest memory I have of this is taking a toy sewing machine apart. I can't remember if it was working properly when I started—it was back in the third grade—but I do recall that when I got done with it, I had a leftover piece and it no longer sewed. That didn't stop me.

I should have thought about that incident a bit last year, when a friend gave me an old serger to try to fix. But she was going to give it to the Salvation Army anyway, so I had nothing to lose. When I plugged it in, it hummed and then made a jamming noise. I couldn't turn the wheel. Slowly, I took it apart, removing more and more pieces, trying to find what was causing the lockup. I now have a large box full of serger parts, including the main body of the serger, which still won't move. I should just toss the whole thing, but one day when I am completely bored I might try again.

I have successfully tinkered with my sewing machines. One notable time was when the wheel on the left side caught a spool of thread while I was sewing. Eventually the entire spool was wrapped around the wheel, and it got stuck. I unstuck it by removing the wheel and yanking all the thread out.

I have also made improvements to sewing machine feet. Some are simple, such as drawing a line on a clear plastic foot to act as a quarter-inch seam guide. And then there was the time I decided I wanted a foot that would allow me to couch thread down while free-motion stitching. One company made a foot that would do that, but not for the machine I owned. I bought the foot, exchanged parts of it with another foot that did fit on my machine, and then realized that my machine did not do a zigzag, so the whole adventure was misguided, and I had wasted about fifty dollars.

On the positive side, I have improved thread racks that didn't work by removing parts and attaching other parts onto them. In one case, I took an old plastic thread stand that had a tension disk that didn't do anything but let the thread fly out of it and replaced the disk with a closed plastic circle from one of my kids' toys. I stuck the thing on top of my longarm with sticky foam tape. It will never come off. Before this effort, I was using a thread stand I had fashioned out of a coat hanger.

My thinking is that if the broken item will not explode, flood the house with water, or electrocute someone, it's worth taking a shot at fixing it myself. Unless, of course, I'll make it worse. I did kill an iPod last month. In my defense, it was already broken; I thought if I replaced the rechargeable battery, I might be able to get it working again. Unfortunately, while replacing the battery, I broke a piece off that appears to be important, and I don't solder well enough to fix it. I was bereft. Because I had had it engraved with "Robbi Joy Eklow, Goddess of the Last Minute," I was emotionally attached to it. Brian tried to make me feel better by pointing out all of the things I've repaired, and this was the first thing he knew about that I had made worse. (He didn't remember the time I shook my slide projector to see if dust was causing the funny sound it was making. The lenses fell out and broke on the floor. Now I do my lectures using a digital projector.) I sold the broken iPod on eBay, borrowed one from my daughter for a while, and then my husband bought me a new one for Valentine's Day.

When I was at the computer store, I was telling a clerk about my misadventure with the battery, and he told me that he's never tried to do this repair himself. He just buys a whole new iPod. I was surprised, but according to an article I read, that mentality is common nowadays—people don't repair, they buy new.

Most of us with sewing machines have, at one time, been told by the dealer not to mess around with the insides of it. We were allowed to clean the dust out of it, but that was it. We were told *not* to mess around with the bobbin tension, an easy adjustment. Heaven forbid we actually open up the cover and look on the inside. I think some of the repair people feel that we will create more problems for *them* if we mess around; they'll have to try to fix what we did. It's sad, because it feels so good to fix something yourself. I still have warm thoughts about the sewing-machine dealer in another state who rescued me one Christmas when my machine stopped working in the middle of a quilt that was promised as a present. Not only did he tell me how to remove the cover and pull thread out of the tension mechanism, solving the problem, he sold me the repair manual for the machine.

Longarm quilters learn to do adjustments and repairs on their machines. It's not easy to bring a twelve-foot-long object into the repair shop, and house calls aren't that available.

I am currently trying to get a repair part for a foot control for another of my machines. The machine is out of warranty, and a replacement foot control will cost close to a hundred dollars. I talked to a representative of the manufacturer at a big quilt show last year, and he told me the repair part is less than twenty dollars and said to contact him to buy it. When I did so, someone else answered the email and suggested a better repair is to buy a new foot control. No, a better repair is to try to fix it myself and then to buy a new foot control if this one is still broken. It's a simple sewing machine; it's not likely I'll kill the machine if I fix the foot control. And I'll feel *so* self-sufficient.

I have saved money that is better spent on fabric by fixing household appliances. Our dishwasher rack is now held together with two twist ties. I have replaced all of the insides of every toilet in the house. I installed two sump pumps in the basement. I did not fix the furnace, because of my not-blowing-up policy; that was better left to a professional.

I'm not alone in this. There are people who buy brand-new things, take them apart to see what's inside, and then post the pictures on the internet. At least I wait until something is broken before I take it apart.

The Printer That Is Entirely Too Large

My favorite way to design a quilt is to use Adobe Illustrator and then print out the pattern full size on my architectural inkjet printer. My printer is thirty-six inches wide, so the sheets can be three feet by four feet before I have to tape them together. The printer was originally used by architects, and although it is so slow I often fall asleep waiting for it to print, I'm sure the original owners were delighted that they no longer had to draw each blueprint with a pencil. To them, waiting half an hour was nothing compared to taking a week to draw a parking garage.

People keep asking me how they can buy a printer like mine, and I just tell them to look on eBay and see what they can find. That's where I got mine. However, when this model came out, users would feed it large sheets of paper. The newer printers (and by newer I mean anything less than twenty years old or so) use rolls of paper. Large sheets are no longer easy to find. And my unit did *not* come with the roll-feed accessory. It took about six months to find large sheets of paper. Of course, a week after finding the proper paper, I saw another auction on eBay for just the roll feed. Now I use rolls.

I also had to find a special cable to connect the old printer to my new computer. It took about a year before

I had everything together. For me, it was worth the effort, because I can design something and print it out the same day, full size, without having to drive somewhere and pay by the square foot. (However, I do use a blueprint service when I make copies for use in my classrooms. Making twenty copies of anything, at half an hour per copy, would not be a good use of my time or sanity. I have to babysit the printer, cut the paper off the roll myself, and then tell it to go on to the next page.)

To me it's like the difference between having a word processor and using a pencil.

But these large printers can be a pain for home users. One day the printouts started looking very funny. I opened up the cover. The belt that moves the ink station along was shredded. I immediately called the manufacturer to order a replacement belt. The lovely woman on the other end forgot to ask me if I had a clue how to install it. About half an hour later, it dawned on me that this was not going to be simple. In fact, the owner's manual said it was for qualified technicians only. Hmmm. I ordered a repair manual, on a CD. When everything arrived, I was all set. First, I looked in the index, "replace drive belt," page 6–67. That would be page 67, in Chapter 6. On that page it said "Step #1, Remove ink station, page 5–51." That would be page 51, Chapter 5. On page 51, of Chapter 5, it said "Step 1, Remove ribbon cable, page 4–32. . . ."

Now, I have to tell you that the belt only cost $15, and the manual only cost $15. The ribbon cable, which was some piece of electronic wiring, would cost $150 if I broke it. I had to pause. I called the blueprint place. How much would it cost for them to print my pattern from scratch? Two dollars. Ah, that was cheap. I wasn't sure why I hadn't tried them in the first place ... oh, I know, I didn't know they existed when I bought the printer. Knowing that even though the printer would cost $4,000 to replace brand new, and I had spent $1,500 to get this one, it would really only cost $2 to get a new pattern printed for the class I had to teach the next week.

Armed with that knowledge, I was able to go to page 4–32, and read "Step 1: Remove the lid: Page 3–21." Yes, I had to move completely backwards through the entire repair manual and dismantle the entire printer to replace this one part—and I did manage to replace it. Apparently, it's a lot of work for professionals too, because the "refurbished" units on eBay do not seem to have new belts installed. I'm betting they don't feel like going backwards through the repair manual page by page, either.

Tattoos

You would be surprised how many quilters have tattoos, have kids with tattoos, or both. I certainly was, over the ten years I contemplated getting ink.

I started thinking about getting a tattoo when I turned forty. There were many drawbacks, besides the oddity of it back then, so I began asking other quilters what they thought about the idea. My favorite response was from an art quilter who said she had considered getting one but didn't want to set a bad example for her son. I set aside the tattoo idea and got my ears double pierced instead, which I thought was pretty daring, until another quilter friend told me her mother—retired and living in Florida—went to the mall with her friends and got another set of ear piercings whenever she got bored.

I kept asking quilters about tattoos, and they started showing me theirs. One quilter I met at a show in Duluth, Minnesota, had "Quilting Forever" on a banner, with wings, on her left shoulder. Another, my personal favorite, had portraits of her grandchildren on her calves and thighs. I wonder if she'll eventually be completely covered in ink as the kids get older and she has to keep updating her gallery. Way more interesting than lining up the school portraits on the piano as we did.

My husband likes to coddle our college kids by doing their laundry when they visit. He thinks that any clothes lying on the floor in their bedrooms are in need of cleaning; he doesn't quite get that they use the floor as the main storage area. One afternoon, he mentioned that it would be nice if the kids would empty their pockets before putting their pants in the laundry (meaning, of course, on the floor). I suggested that they do their own laundry, and a loud argument ensued.

Suddenly, Brian said, "So, Sam, where is your tattoo?" The room went silent.

Sam said, "What tattoo? I don't have a tattoo."

"Here is a note that was in your pocket that says: 'Make tattoo appointment.'"

"That was for my *boyfriend.*"

The argument about the laundry started up again. Sam left the room in a huff, Brian followed her, and they had a little chat.

Later that night, Brian and I went out for coffee. "Sam has a tattoo," I said.

"No, she said that was her boyfriend's," Brian answered. "And I believe her. Anyway, how are you going to find out?"

I told him that from the look on her face, it was obvious she had a tattoo. And I was her mother; I'd find out somehow.

The very next morning, my son Josh and I were eating breakfast when Sam came downstairs in a teeny string bikini and headed for the backyard to sunbathe. I hooked my thumb around one of the strings, exposing her left buttock, and her tattoo: two hearts. "Josh, look at the tattoo on your sister!" Sam was so mortified that she forgot to complain, and Josh started laughing. I told Sam that I wouldn't tell her father she had a tattoo, if she promised not to *ever* yell at me like she had the day before, and she had to be really nice to me the rest of the summer. She agreed. Later, I told my husband that Sam had a tattoo but not to mention it because I was blackmailing her. I think I spilled the beans to both of them the next day.

That summer, I was busy designing quilt fabric when Sam came over, examined a computer graphic I was doing, and asked if she could use it for a tattoo on her foot.

"No."

"Why not?"

I was busy thinking about whether the fabric company would be upset if her foot "debuted" before the fabric came out. And who really owned the copyright to the motif, me or them? I'd have to talk to them about it. In the meantime, Sam said she really didn't need my permission anyway. Why did she ask then? She wanted my opinion, she said. I think she was hoping I'd say, "What a great idea! I'll treat!" She tried this with a belly-button piercing, which I did pay for—I think mainly because my husband had said "no," and he always says "yes" to Sam. So I got to be the good guy on that one. Also, it looked cute, and she has a flat stomach. Her nose piercing looks cute too,

although I didn't pay for that, having expressed my opinion that it was gross.

Sam got the quilt fabric motif done on her foot, and
apparently it hurt quite a bit. I sent a picture of it to Ruby,
the company's fabric stylist, who was amused and hung it up
in her office. Eventually they named the fabric line "Tatou"
after Sam's tattoo. We arranged the motif in two different
designs, in several colorways. How many people have fabric
that matches their tattoos? In the end, I was flattered that
Sam would want something I designed on her foot for the
rest of her life. Quite a nice tribute if you think about it.
Weird, but nice.

Assuming that Josh would want a tattoo as well, I told
him that if he got the traditional "Mom" tattoo—a banner
on a heart—that I'd treat.

As I faced my fiftieth birthday, I thought about getting my
own tattoo again. Most of my misgivings were fading away.
At fifty, there was little chance I'd be interviewing for a corporate job. At this point, being a professional artist probably wouldn't preclude having a tattoo. Plus, I could probably
hide it if necessary. I thought my parents might be upset,
but at seventy-two, my mother is doing a lot of things that
I don't approve of either, so that issue has gone away. Also,
Sam told me that her grandmother thinks her tattoos are
cute. (Though my mother thinks everything Sam does is
cute—me, not so much.) My stepfather would probably be
upset by a tattoo, but if it were in the right place, I could
hide it by wearing pants.

People asked if I wanted to be an eighty-year-old lady with a saggy tattoo. I'll be an eighty-year-old lady with saggy everything. At fifty, I'm rarely, if ever, mistaken for a twenty-something anyway.

Someone warned me that if you get a tattoo, you can't get an MRI because of the metal in the ink. I talked to a quilter who is also a nurse, who has tattoos. (Again, not as uncommon as you would think.) This discussion took place while waiting for a plane with a group of quilters after a quilt show; everyone who had a tattoo was sharing it with the group. At least the ones they could show with discretion. The nurse told me that only prison tattoos precluded MRIs, so as long as I avoided going to prison for my ink, I'd be okay.

I did, however, decide to get the tattoo on my right calf. I was thinking that my calves won't sag that much. I could wear cropped pants and show it off. I could wear socks and hide it. The left calf was out, as I'm starting to get varicose veins.

The last decision was to choose a design that I could live with until I'm eighty and have saggy calves. I thought about a bracelet of spirals for a few months. Then one day, while I was having my grey hair colored, I was telling my stylist about all the objects I've collected with the word "Joy" on them.

It started several years ago, when I found Christmas ornaments on clearance that spelled "Joy," each letter made out of a translucent plastic, covered with fake sugar to look like pieces of candy. I hung them on a boring light in the dining room. The next year I found Christmas stocking holders that spelled "Joy" and grabbed those. January is a great time to find things with "Joy" on them, leftover from the Christmas rush of "Peace, Love, and Joy." I was describing my coffee cup, "Joy" in Chinese on one side, in English on the other. Aha! I should get "Joy" for my tattoo! In Chinese! But I can't actually read Chinese. Maybe in Hebrew, since I am Jewish. Maybe there is even a symbol for that, similar to the "chai" character that symbolizes "life." I used to have a necklace like that.

I called Sam and told her my idea. "Mom, you are Jewish. You aren't supposed to get tattoos anyway; don't you think one in Hebrew would be odd?" Yes, perhaps. "Britney Spears got one in Hebrew and everyone made fun of her." Well, I *certainly* do *not* want to be mistaken for Ms. Spears. Hebrew was out. English was in.

Sam called my husband that night to suggest that she and my son would treat me to the tattoo for my birthday. They would come home to witness the installation.

A big quilt show in Chicago was scheduled for the weekend after my birthday, the first chance the kids could come home. One of the events at the show is a reception for members of the internet list Quiltart. During the reception, we customarily have a Tiara Parade. Grown women make tiaras, show them off during the parade, and then winners are chosen to receive coveted tiara-shaped brooches collected by the hostess. I had never won a tiara, even though I had been participating for about eight years. Sam decided to create our tiaras and come to the reception. Then, we would meet Josh at the tattoo parlor, get our tattoos, and the kids would return to school.

Sam and I won "First Runner-Up," or "Second Place" as her boyfriend pointed out. I was happy to have finally won something, even if I had to bring in a ringer. While we celebrated, my quilting friends opined on which font to have "Joy" done on my calf.

We called Josh, then headed for the tattoo parlor. First we had to stop at the bank and get some cash. Apparently tattoo parlors do not take credit cards—maybe because they can't repossess the tattoo if the card turns out to be stolen.

Josh decided he'd get the "Mom" tattoo as part of the festivities. I had promised to treat him to that, but I thought it was a little unfair that my "Joy" tattoo—my birthday present from the kids—would cost less than I was spending on them. "Mom, we are getting you a present you will have forever," they assured me. Yes, that was true. Besides, how many mothers get to label their sons?

Josh's artist got going on his tattoo, while mine redrew the design I had brought in. Finally we got started; both kids came in to watch and entertain me. It didn't hurt nearly as much as I thought it would. In fact, when Sandy, the tattoo artist, did a little test poke, I asked her if she had actually done anything. After a while, it did burn a bit; in the end though, it wasn't that bad. The kids and I told Sandy stories about our family while she did the ink, and she declared we were a crazy family, in a good way. We had fun. The kids informed me that you tip about twenty dollars per tattoo, and we all paid up. Sam offered to get another tattoo in honor of the event, but luckily the parlor was closing.

That night, Josh and I stayed up late, until it was time to remove the bandages, examine our art, and clean it off properly. We had a nice conversation about Josh's plans for grad school and beyond. Truly a bonding experience. My husband admired our new ink but said we could not possibly talk him into getting any and went to sleep.

My son's girlfriend's mother is a quilter. And a nurse, and she has tattoos too! We decided to meet, for the first time, at the quilt show that Sunday. I wore cropped pants, in order to show off my new art acquisition. At the show, I spent a lot of time saying, "This is my son's girlfriend's mother! She's a quilter too! And look at my new tattoo! I turned fifty this week!" My new friend reminded me to moisturize the tattoo every so often—very important for healing. What better way to spend the day than with another quilter, at a quilt show, telling each other how much we like the other's kid, and admiring our ink.

CHAPTER TWO

Home Is Where the Quilts Are

Note to Self: Not All Quilts Hang on Walls

We'd like to interrupt this book, devoted to the art of making art quilts, to bring you a public service announcement: "Quilts can actually be made to cover beds. And you can even sleep with them." We now return you to your reading about artsy-fartsy quilts.

You may be wondering why I had to point out the obvious fact that quilts can be made for beds. The reason is that many of us who have made art quilts for far too long have forgotten this simple fact. I myself had this problem. Last week, I went to Target in order to buy some new pillows. We were having a houseguest, and I wanted some fresh pillows, since I couldn't remember if we still had any extras or if the kids had taken them away to college. My own pillows are getting pretty flat too, so my agenda included pillows for myself. (My husband thought that I had some extra pillows on the sofa where I like to nap. He suggested I look there, but I couldn't find them, so he is wrong—as he is so often—or I looked on the wrong couch, since I do tend to nap all over the house.)

While I was debating about whether I should get expensive pillows or go with the five-dollar jobbies, I remembered that I should probably look at sheets, since I can't stand the sheets we have now. We don't have a supply of extra sheets. I managed to clean out the linen closet sometime last year and tossed all the old ones, leaving us with a set of flannel sheets that are now wearing out, as they tend to do; some red cotton ones that Brian bought and that I hate because I like red, but not to sleep on; and the gold ones that came with the comforter that is on our bed. I don't like the comforter either. The end cap had some nice sheets with a high thread count, but what color to pick? The walls of our bedroom are peach, the carpet blue. A long time ago, I had a comforter that had peach and blue in it, and I liked that comforter. I started to wonder where it was. I could get blue to match the carpet that I don't really like anymore, as it is twenty years old, or peach to match the walls, which were painted about fifteen years ago, or tan to match the comforter that I don't like. I started thinking about the idea of replacing the carpet and repainting the walls—should I just wait until then to replace the sheets? The fifty-dollar sheet purchase was now expanding to several thousand dollars. However, I blame the sheets, because I really do need sheets soon, so I can get rid of the bags under my eyes. I haven't been sleeping well lately; I get too hot, and then I'm too cold. Menopause.

I put the blue sheets in the cart. Blue is the color I tend to gravitate to; it's calming. Then, I noticed that they make sheets for thicker mattresses. These were for eighteen-inch mattresses; they also had sheets for twenty-inch mattresses. How thick is our mattress? I don't remember buying special sheets, but the mattress is thick. When we got the new one, I had to start using the step stool that came with the four-poster bed to climb in.

I thought about calling Brian and asking him to measure the mattress for me, but then we'd probably have to have a discussion about why we need new sheets when we have these perfectly fine red ones, and I'd have to remind him how much I hate them. Since I was hoping he'd cook dinner, I didn't want to bother with that. I put the twenty-inch sheets into the cart and wandered farther down the aisle, thinking maybe they'd have a comforter I would like. I don't like the way the one we have feels. It's too thick, but it doesn't weigh enough. It doesn't feel good to curl up in it. I was looking for a thin comforter that had some heft. And would match my blue carpet and peach walls. It would only have to last a while until I got going on the room rehab.

I couldn't find anything I liked at Target. I thought about looking at Macy's; they have better stuff. I certainly deserve to have nice bed linens. And maybe they'd have better color selections. And something that would feel more "quilty," like that quilt that Jeri Riggs put on the guest bed when I stayed at her house. Wait a minute . . . I'm a quilter. I have fabric, *lots* of it, even in peach and blue. And I have batting; a nice wool would do well. *And*, hey, I have a *long-arm sewing machine*. I use it for art quilts but, excuse me, they are designed for people who make *BIG QUILTS!!! Oh, MY GOODNESS!* I even have a line of my own fabric I could make a quilt out of. . . .

I put the sheets back, loaded the cart with a whole bunch of pillows, threw in a Bon Jovi DVD for Brian to thank him for making dinner, and left the store.

It's not like I have never made a bed quilt. Okay, it *is* like I have never made a bed quilt. I started one back in the nineties: an Ocean Waves, machine pieced but hand quilted. It's still not done. I got bored with the hand quilting. And last year I even quilted a queen-sized quilt out of the fabrics I designed for Cranston. Because of the time frame allowed for making that quilt, to be used for publicity, I couldn't piece it myself. I had the fabric sent to another quilter, Retta Warehime, who pieced it in return for a promise that I would quilt a quilt for her. (Retta, if you are reading this, send me your quilt.) She shipped it back to me, I quilted it—quickly, as mostly they were interested in seeing the fabric—and then tried to put a regular binding on it. I screwed that up, so I fused the binding on. (Not that comfy to sleep with, I admit.) When Cranston was done with it, I put it on my bed and admired it. At last, a bed quilt of my own. And that night, Brian carefully folded it up, put it on the sofa, and went to sleep with the comforter I don't like. I asked him why we weren't using my quilt. "Oh, that's for the *bed?* I thought it was another of your quilts headed for a show and you were just keeping it on the bed while you looked for a shipping box."

My son Josh was feeling displaced after I painted his room and turned it into a guestroom, so I put the quilt on his futon/sofa. When Brian was making up the futon with the new pillows, he again folded up the quilt and put it back in our room. He still didn't understand that it's a bed quilt. I mentioned to my daughter, Sam, that I was going to give the Cranston quilt to Josh for his graduation. She said that I'd then have to make *her* a quilt, and *he* shouldn't get this one, as it matches her tattoo. Which it does. But I'm *not* going to start making bed quilts. Okay, I might.

Until then, I'm going to see what's on sale at Crate & Barrel.

Sharpies Forever

If I ever go completely crazy and the authorities have to break into my house, they won't find forty-two cats or a room full of garbage. They are more likely to find five thousand dried-up Sharpies and notes written on every surface.

Sharpies are permanent markers that write on just about anything—and I've been testing the limits.

One thing that annoys me about modern manufacturing is the lack of clear directions written directly on products. For example, my printer has an I/O switch, or maybe it's 1/0. I don't know, and I can't remember whether ON is O or I, and if ON *is* O, what does the "I" mean? The printer goes to sleep after a while, and half the time I can't tell if it's I or O. (Or 1 or 0.) After having to stand there several times while it restarts unnecessarily, I pulled out a Sharpie and wrote "OFF" on the right side of the switch.

Laser printers never come with good enough labeling to show you how to feed paper in when doing two-sided printing. Every printer in our house now has the directions plainly written, in Sharpie, right on the front of the paper tray. It's not a classy look, but one can only do so many trial and error tests before one starts to complain about wasting paper.

I write all over household appliances too.

My daughter saw the microwave I keep in my dye studio. She thought I was down there eating snacks and hiding them from the rest of the family. So, I wrote "NO FOOD!" right on the door. Another dyeing hint: When you open a new dye jar, write the date on the lid. Then you know how long that jar lasted—good info to have on hand when it's time to reorder. Also, when the dyed fabric is coming out the wrong color, you can tell if it's because the dye powder is from the last century.

My new clothes dryer has a lint filter that could go in two different ways: one way being correct, the other way getting stuck and refusing to come out again. I drew an arrow pointing into the dryer right on the vent. (Which, now that I think about it, makes no sense to anyone else. How will they know what the arrow means? I'd better go back and relabel it to say, "This side in.") The arrow on the dryer dial was hard to read; easier now that there is a big arrow drawn right on it.

Because I am left handed, I get confused about which way to turn things that roll, like can openers. I mark arrows on those too.

One of my sewing machines has ambiguous markings to indicate which way to push a lever to drop the feed dogs. I wrote "up" and "down" on the machine bed. If I were taller, I might have noticed that there were directions molded right into the lever. Again, that problem with the molding thing. I have a Bernina on loan, and they asked me please not to write on it, so I've refrained, but I have drawn lines 1/4 inch away from the center point on one of the clear machine feet. It is very easy to slide the fabric under the foot and line up the edge with the marking.

Some quilters make elaborate labels for the backs of their quilts. I've seen some impressive ones with the washing instructions, the history of the quilt, even poems. Not me. I find a scrap of fabric that already has WonderUnder fused onto the back, cut out a rectangle with pinking shears, write my name, address, phone number, and the quilt name with a Sharpie, and then iron that thing right onto the back of the quilt. If it comes loose, I iron it back down again. I figure the day I make fancy labels is the day that the phone company will change my area code again.

Our local grocery store chain lets you "pay with your finger." First they scan your right and left index fingers, and you give them a seven-digit number. When you are ready to pay for your groceries, you hit the button that says "pay by finger," let it scan your finger, and then punch in your seven-digit number. Someone was already using our home phone number, so I used my cell phone number. I can never remember my number; I thought this would be a good impetus to memorize it. Nope. I had to tape my business card to the phone, since it had a black body and I couldn't find a white opaque Sharpie. The business card fell off a while ago. What I do now is find the screen on the phone that gives me my number. This takes a while, and it is embarrassing. For some reason, I can remember the phone number of my college dorm room from thirty years ago but not my current cell phone number.

When I got my lime green iBook back in 2000, I wrote my name and address on the plastic on the bottom. The iBook looks like a child should own it, and the labeling fits right in. My kids teased me, and then one of them lost an expensive calculator. If they weren't too cool to have their name on their stuff, they wouldn't have had to spend another hundred bucks on a calculator. Would they?

My kids are just lucky that they were born when I could still remember things, because if they were babies now, it's very likely I would marker their foreheads with their names. I'll have to remember that when they start bringing grandkids around.

The Editor

You know that part of your subconscious that listens to everything you say and watches everything you do, and then tells you that you are an idiot? I have named her "THE EDITOR." I use all caps, not to shout, but to distinguish THE EDITOR who lives in my head, from an actual person with the job title of editor who carefully goes through what I write and fixes it so that whether or not *she* thinks I'm an idiot, the people who read what I write think I'm brilliant. (Or as THE EDITOR says to tell you, at least mediocre.)

Please tell me you have your own version of THE EDITOR, or else I'll have to make an appointment with a therapist. (THE EDITOR is telling me to stop being so needy and pathetic.)

THE EDITOR is out in full strength when I start a run of workshop teaching. Usually the first day I can hear myself talk through the same filter I myself use on other teachers when I take a workshop. This is not good, because my conscious brain can be very snotty—how bad do you think my unconscious and uncontrolled EDITOR can be? After a few days, she wanders off and goes shopping if it is a quilt show.

THE EDITOR loves it when I'm trying to write. She sits there on my left shoulder, like one of those angel/devil pairs you see on TV characters trying to convince them how to act. Except THE EDITOR does not have a counterpart; if she did, it would be my subconscious telling me that I write wonderfully and to please go on. Instead, in order to write creatively, I have to wait until THE EDITOR goes to sleep or gets distracted by music.

Now that I'm writing about it, perhaps it's just the difference between being fully conscious and being in a state of "Flow." Left brain, right brain. . . .

Okay, since THE EDITOR is still awake, she's telling me to stay on point. Here's the point: I want a real editor to follow me around all day. Let's suppose that I'm having a conversation and say something dumb, as I usually do. I want the real editor to turn back time, fix my sentence, and then encourage me to go on. I want her to assure my students that, indeed, I know what I'm talking about. But alas, I don't have an editor willing to do that. Instead, I have to bumble along on my own.

I just had an idea. My daughter might not have a job right away when she graduates from college . . . maybe I can hire her to be my personal assistant and do all that. Wait, I just thought of something, she already does all this for free. I *do* have an editor. She's just been away at college.

Ann Landers

Long ago and far away, someone wrote in to either Ann Landers or her twin sister Abby, the advice columnists, and asked if she should go to medical school. She would be fifty by the time she graduated, and she was wondering if it was too late. Ann or Abby said that in fours years she'd be fifty anyway, with or without the doctorate. Now, I'm sure I have half of this story wrong, but that doesn't matter. The point is that time passes no matter what.

When Samantha was in kindergarten, she took gymnastics classes twice a week. Since they were a few hours long, I sometimes went grocery shopping or ran other short errands during the classes. Sam noticed that I was the only mother who would leave; the other mothers stayed and watched. I decided I'd better stick around too, although I did tell Sam that she shouldn't be taking the class just so I could watch her—if she didn't find it entertaining, she didn't have to do it. Nonetheless, she seemed to have more fun if she could look up at me in the second-floor waiting room, looking back at her out the window.

I started bringing a Mariner's Compass wall hanging along. I was putting it together with an early paper-piecing method. I had drawn templates on freezer paper, cut them out, ironed them on fabric, and sewed along the edges of the freezer paper, which then had to be torn out. I used Sam's class time to cut out the templates and later to pull off the paper.

There was a clique of mothers in the group, which did not include me. That didn't bother me a bit, as their main topic of conversation seemed to be how their yeast infections were being cured by eating more yogurt. I am not making that up—they talked about it for months. Another mother, also not in the clique, seemed to be only capable of saying, in an annoying voice, "Shawn Michael, stop doing that!" I sat quietly and worked on my quilt. One day one of the cliquey women came over to see what I was doing. I told her I was making a wall hanging. She said, "Oh, nice! I would love to do some crafts, but I never have the time." I did not reply with the advice that if she would work on a quilt while she discussed her yeast infection, she would have something finished by the end of the semester. Instead, I smiled and wondered what it was that Shawn Michael insisted on doing every day.

Vases All Over the Place

I have a large collection of vases and decorative glass. For many years, I concentrated on making still-life quilts; these items were my "models." I have a few vases that were inherited from my mother-in-law, Eileen, who apparently also liked collecting vases, most notably a giant, white, porcelain specimen. She also left us an ugly porcelain clock, inherited from her own mother. (I proposed that the only reason Eileen had it was because no one else in the family wanted it, but my husband didn't buy that.) Visiting relatives have also brought us vases from Sweden. My friend Lynne sometimes sees an odd vase or bottle and grabs it for me, which would explain the two "leaning bottles" in the collection.

Every once in a while a quilter remembers that I do still lifes and brings me a gift at a lecture. This can be problematic when I'm about to get on an airplane to go back home, but so far, none of them have been broken.

The collection got noticeably bigger when the Pier One outlet was only a few miles away. Although I limited my purchases to clearance items less than three dollars, I managed to bring home about twenty.

The accumulation got worse when I started amassing teapots and pitchers—actually, anything that held liquid.

I would say that at the peak of the collection I had about a hundred items.

Luckily, I also have several china buffets. Now, please note that I said "buffets," not hutches. Buffets are table height; hutches have shelves. I happen to have four china buffets but, oddly enough, haven't collected china—at least not the kind that you would use to serve food. My collection of still-life objects was spread around the buffets, and when they got full, I installed a decorative bookshelf in the dining room. The living and dining rooms were filled with these objects; the good stuff mixed in with the fifty-cent teacups bought at a garage sale.

Although this collection takes over the dining and living rooms, I tend to forget that "normal" people use these objects to make tea or hold flowers. My vases are usually empty because I'm allergic to flowers. My daughter is not allergic, so she borrows one or two if she has a romantic boyfriend.

Last summer, I discovered that all of the chairs in our dining room were broken. My son's friends grabbed them to use in the kitchen when they were over playing poker, and they lean on the back legs. Bad for chairs. We went to the Amish furniture store to see if they had any chairs we could order. We found a cherry Arts and Crafts style dining set: six chairs, table (with four leaves), giant buffet, and hutch (the kind with shelves and a big mirror). It was half price. It was ours. But we didn't want it delivered until the college boys left for the year. And then we further delayed delivery because I was teaching so much I wasn't in town long enough to clean off all the other shelves and make room for the hutch.

Finally one weekend, when I was afraid the store would keep our deposit and give someone else the dining set, I cleared out the collection. Cheap vases went into the recycle bin. Better vases went to resale shops. Of course, we kept vases we bought when we traveled. (I had even forgotten I owned some of them.) Everything we inherited stayed too— even the ugly stainless steel ones from Brian's grandfather. Those are in the buffet, behind doors. Safe, but out of sight. Until I need one to model for me.

Does a Quilter Need a Spinning Wheel?

I accidentally bought a spinning wheel last year. By "accident," I mean that it was unplanned and unexpected, not that I crashed into it and they forced me to buy it. Although that would have been a more logical explanation. We all have unplanned purchases, especially when there is a sale, but one hopes that some logic is involved. As in, "This is something I can use. And it's a great price." I seem to be stuck on the "And it's a great price" part.

This was not the first time I bought some fiber-related object that I have no idea how to use. When vacationing in Italy, I discovered a yarn shop in the Piazza San Lorenzo. I didn't knit, but I thought I might couch some of the yarns into a quilt.

Thinking you might use some non-quilting item in a quilt is a slippery slope. You can't just have *one* thing in the quilt, you have to have lots of them, or else it looks stupid. This is how I ended up with a large collection of charms back in the nineties. I only stopped collecting those when the vendor stopped showing up at quilt shows. But I have never used a charm in a quilt.

When I stopped buying charms, I started buying porcelain buttons. I did use about ten of those in a quilt; of course,

I had to buy about a hundred more before I stopped with that streak. I think we quilters get suckered into buying a lot of something at the same time because we are used to doing that with fabric. We buy one of something, that's just a thing; then two of something, that's a pair; three is a collection; four is the start of a stash; five hundred is a museum.

Thus, when I got to Italy, I bought about twenty skeins of yarn: one in each color. There was also this wooden thing that spun around and had arms that extended and compressed. It stood on a wooden stand with a spike coming out of the top of it. The proprietor didn't speak enough English to explain what it was, and my Italian was limited to asking if she spoke English. (Actually, what I said was, "Do I speak English?" to which the answer was yes, and then we couldn't go any further.) So I bought the wooden thing. My whole bill was only fifty bucks, as the American dollar was strong against the lira. This was not a bad way to spend money on souvenirs.

The yarn turned out to be even a bigger bargain than I thought; when I got home, I discovered that Italian yarn sells for about four times what I had paid. I consider the spinny thing to have been free. I displayed the yarn in a bowl, next to the spinning thing, on a buffet in our living room.

When I actually started knitting, years later, I discovered that I had bought a swift, which one uses to hold a hank of yarn while winding a ball. That model sells for over sixty dollars in the U.S. now, and I'm very glad I have it. I do use it.

I have an affinity for wooden objects that spin around and, thus, the spinning wheel has always appealed to me—aesthetically, if not as an object that I might use.

Brian and I were in the city for the weekend, to stay at our condo. I had been saving up to buy an iPhone, and we had just come back from the Apple store, empty handed. I wasn't impressed enough with the iPhone to actually buy it, geeky as it was, because, truth be told, I don't actually like cell phones. I just wanted it for the iPod part: the part that would play music and connect to the internet, giving me access to my email all day long and everywhere that cell phone service could be had. The phone was going to cost $600, plus $60 a month for the service plan, for two years. Total: $2,040. Plus tax. I passed.

We decided to take a bus and go to dinner somewhere in the city. We don't have a parking space at our condo. It's a long story you don't want to hear, trust me, but we are waiting for someone in the building to move out and free up a space. We are at the top of the waiting list—have been there for four years. So our practice is to drive into the city during the day on Friday, park the car on a side street, and then leave it there until we want to go home. Otherwise we have to park far away, and I'm not walking alone at night to get to the car.

Anyway, we were taking the bus to dinner. "How about stopping at Arcadia Knitting on the way?" I asked. "I could use some stitch holders."

I like Arcadia, and I like to knit at the condo. It

doesn't take up much room, and I can knit while Brian drives back and forth from our "real" house. Brian agreed, and off we went. It turned out that the spinning wheel I had admired in the window was on sale. The Ashford Joy. Now, Joy is my middle name. I like to collect things with "Joy" on them. I have a lot of stuff that says "Joy." Brian even bought laundry detergent called "Joyful Expressions" last week because he thought it sounded like the name of my first book, and also included "Joy." (We then agreed that our daughter, Sam, should only buy generic cleaning products at Sam's Club so they have her name on them.)

With the money that I hadn't spent on the iPhone, the appeal of buying something that was on the opposite end of the technology spectrum was great; in fact, instead of being the latest thing, a spinning wheel is probably the "oldest thing." I remembered how happy I'd been that I bought the swift in Italy. This spinning wheel could look very pretty in my living room, just being there. It didn't have to be useful, it could just *be*.

Using my non-cutting-edge cell phone, I called Kathleen, a friend who has a spinning wheel and knows how to use it, and whose judgment I trust. "Kathleen, the Ashford Joy is on sale. Thirty percent off. Is this a good price? If yes, should I get one pedal or two?" Yes, it was a good price and one pedal would be the way to go in her opinion. I didn't understand the explanation, but I knew Kathleen wouldn't lie to me.

I got the wheel and the custom carrying case, thus wiping out the beneficial effects of the discount. But that is beside the point. I was entering one of the oldest clubs in the world; the world of people who spin fiber to be knitted or woven into cloth. Way better than an iPhone, which would just introduce me to people who happened to have my cell phone number.

The spinning wheel was accompanied by a free spinning lesson. The teacher was very young and very kind. It was a private lesson; I think she was practicing on me before she taught a roomful of people. I told her at the start that I also teach, but quilting, and I understand that things can be complicated. Good thing I warned her, because I am also a verbal person. I wasn't swearing, but I did say "oops" every two minutes when I got the wheel spinning backwards. I have to say, spinning is sort of like learning how to ride a unicycle. The pedal is attached directly; you can't coast; and if you pedal at the wrong time in the spin cycle, it starts going backwards. Also, you have to keep stretching out the fibers as you go. Maybe it's more like riding a unicycle and juggling at the same time.

I wasn't that great at spinning, but it felt wonderful. It had been a long time since I learned how to do something complicated like that. I celebrated by buying some hand-dyed yarn that was heavily discounted. I got four skeins. Then the next day, I realized that I needed more of this yarn and bought two more skeins, and some yarn to knit a purse. So far, the savings I had foreseen were not forthcoming. Especially since I then went to a craft fair and bought some more stuff to spin. And extra spindles. And a few books on spinning.

Brian has failed to point out the folly of the spinning-wheel purchase. I did ask him the next day why he hadn't mentioned that this was an extravagant thing to buy all of a sudden. He said that it wasn't worth arguing about, and he was just happy that our subdivision didn't allow sheep.

The Kids Shall Inherit the Quilts . . .
And Everything Else

I was working on my will and decided to ask the kids who should get my quilts and other collected stuff. Both agreed that they would take care of my quilts and wouldn't sell them at a garage sale. Most of my other stuff, though, they didn't really want. I have a few odd collections, granted, but most of them don't take up much space. I think I will make it so that if they want a quilt, they have to keep one collection for each quilt.

Brian travels a lot. When the kids were little, I would get lonely while he was gone. When he'd come home from an exotic place, like Indianapolis, I'd ask if he brought me anything. The answer was always no, even if he knew they had some neat stuff I would want, like leather purses from faraway Paraguay. That's where they make beautiful tooled bags.

I think that what I really wanted was to know that Brian was missing me while he was gone. When I expressed that thought to him, he began to bring home a present on each trip: a thimble with the name of the place, or maybe a picture. Now, these were not as exciting as you would think, and they certainly didn't fool me into believing he was missing me and spending the odd free evening looking around for a precious trinket to bring home. Brian was getting the thimbles at the airport gift shop, during the few hours he had to bop around after going through security.

The first few thimbles were incredibly boring and cheaply made, usually with a decal or sometimes a glued-on shield, each one the same as the next. I finally declared the thimble collection to be *his*, as he was getting more enjoyment out of it than me. That is when the tide changed and the fun began. The first interesting thimble came from Texas; I brought it home after a layover in Dallas. It's pewter, with an aardvark sitting on the top. You certainly couldn't sew with it.

I showed it to Brian. "Now *this* is really something to collect," I said. "You can't get these just anywhere."

We started looking for thimbles everywhere we went. On a family trip to San Francisco, we snagged several: one, pewter, with a cable car; another, pewter, with the Golden Gate Bridge; and another, carved or, rather, molded plastic, with the painted-lady Victorian houses that San Francisco is known for. We even found an antique thimble at a fabric store in Berkeley. And let us not forget the thimble from Alcatraz.

The kids started collecting them too. Without consulting each other, they brought the same one home from their trips to Washington. Chris, a friend of theirs, brought home a coconut model from Hawaii. Kathleen's husband Mark brought back a very well-made model from Britain. I went to New Zealand, collecting them at every site. Our next-door neighbors got confused and brought home a shot glass from the Catskills. We keep all this stuff in two printer's drawers hanging on the wall—you know, the big, flat drawers with dividers. The shot glass fits in one section, so we kept it.

We have divided the thimbles into categories: Those with architectural items, in pewter, sitting on the top—the ones you couldn't possibly use. The molded ones. The cheap ones with the glued-on shields. We don't believe for a minute any of these were made on site. If the "Made in China" sticker is still on the thimble, we feel that is a bonus.

I started to include slides of the thimble collection in my quilt lecture, and people started giving me thimbles when I visited their guild. One day I noted that the fezzes the Shriners wear during their motor-cycle parade resemble giant thimbles. I bought one on eBay and added it to my lecture, saying that people give me thimbles all the time: here is my Elvis thimble, here is my Seattle Space Needle thimble, here is one given to me by a Shriner . . . and then I would show a slide of a fez. This joke went over very well in Fargo, North Dakota, but in New Zealand, they just stared at me. When the stares continued in other parts of the United States, I reluctantly removed that slide from my lecture. Just because I thought it was hilarious didn't mean I should keep explaining the joke.

One thimble that has eluded me is the one from Newark, New Jersey. I have flown into and out of that airport at least five times. They *never* have a New Jersey thimble. They have shot glasses, spoons, and commemorative plates, but the only thimbles they ever have when I am there say "I Heart New York." I already have that one. I got it at LaGuardia, which is actually *in* New York. Newark is not in New York, so it's a puzzle to me why they don't have their own thimble, perhaps with a flower mounted on top and "Garden State" carved around the bottom.

I'm not saying that the kids have to keep the thimbles displayed in a prominent place in their home after they inherit them; it's fine with me if they live in a shoebox. The thimbles, not the kids. I hope the kids have reasonably large houses (at least bigger than a shoebox) so they can store my other stuff, such as my collection of journals.

I just love buying a blank book every now and again. I have no clue why. It's not that I fill them up with important thoughts. I do most of my writing on my computer. I try to carry around a journal, but my purse is already overloaded. I start out with good intentions, dating the journal, writing on a few pages, then I lose interest until a few months later, when I forget I had the first book going and buy another.

I bought one in Italy in 2000. Every page was dated; it was more of a diary than a journal, if you consider that a diary is predated. I wrote a few things and then, again, abandoned it. I've decided that this behavior is okay if I limit myself to journals that are special, not just cheap notebooks that I buy on sale. If I keep them all on the same shelf and then write a few pages in every one, I have, in fact, created a collection of ephemera related to my life. One day, when I am long dead but still famous (I may be exaggerating here), someone will find my shelf full of journals and be very excited that each book has my signature and some of my writing. At least, that is what I hope for when I reach for that coveted, snazzy new journal, all leather-bound and shiny.

Too Many Books?

I'll bet that you love to read quilting books just as much as I do. I'll further bet that you have another fiber-related book affection. For me, it's knitting, beading, and spinning.

To me, fiber books are a guilty pleasure. My habit started back in the 1960s, when my Uncle Skippy brought my grandmother a book on macramé. She wasn't much interested—her only addiction was knitting—so she passed the book to me. (I was living with her at the time.) Grama, who was only five feet tall, used a footstool with u-shaped legs that formed handles at the top of the stool. I used the handles as a base to tie mounting cords for the macramé projects. She still rested her feet on it, knotted strings and all, until I finished each project and took it off the stool. I did macramé for nearly the next decade; Grama did well to encourage me.

In turn, I try to encourage my children to take up fiber arts by having an extensive library for them to peruse. I'm not sure if it's working, but I've noticed that my daughter does read through some of the quilt books when they are lying on the kitchen table.

I use different excuses to buy fiber books: I had a coupon, the store was having a sale, on Amazon it's almost half price, I needed this book because it has one bit of information that

I can't find anywhere else. I don't know why I bother making excuses. I use the money I earn from teaching to buy the books, Brian never sees the book bills, and he has admitted that he can't tell the difference between a pile of books I've bought and a pile of books that came home with me from the library.

A few months ago, I was "forced" to buy a book because the copy I had out from the library got a bit wet on the top edge. The library insisted that it was completely impossible for me to have overlooked the water damage when I returned it. I was a bit miffed because I don't abuse books. They weren't having it and insisted I replace the book, as it was unusable. I ordered a new one and then traded them. Frankly, I was thinking about buying the book anyway, so the only irritation was the librarian's attitude that I was some dishonest person for not pointing out the damage in the first place. Once I got the damaged book back, I was even more irritated because the only bit of evidence that the book had gotten wet was along the very top of a few pages, in an area lacking any text. The book was certainly not "unreadable."

Quite often I order a book online before I leave for a teaching trip, and the book comes after I'm back from my trip. When this happens, it is not uncommon for me to forget *why* I specifically ordered that one.

I particularly enjoy reading knitting books. I don't knit very well, and I have to admit, if I spent the same amount of money on socks that I do on sock-knitting books, my feet would be very warm. It isn't really about the socks though;

it's about reading the directions and seeing if I understand them. Sometimes I do, sometimes I don't. If not, I can just turn the page and not worry about having to perform the skills called for in the book. I can look at the pictures and enjoy the color and design. Maybe something will bleed over into a quilt design.

My beading books are the same. I like to look at the sparkly colored pictures and try to figure out how to follow the instructions. My husband is very happy that I have never tried to make lampworked beads. It is safer if I am not wielding torches of any form.

I bet most quilters, even if they are more careful about what they buy, have many more books than finished quilts. I no longer feel guilty about that. If I collected murder mysteries, would I feel bad about not going out and killing a few people every time I got a new book? Of *course* not.

My book habit has rubbed off on my son. The public library in the next town loves him, as he used to regularly check out the maximum number of items, which was fifty. They get part of their funding based on circulation. Josh and I buy each other books when we see something that might interest the other person. We both leave reading materials everywhere in the house. When Josh was in third grade, his teacher was completely impressed that he knew the police in Canada are called Mounties. The reason he was familiar with them was because he subscribed to a professional wrestling magazine and there was a tag team called the Mounties. (Two brothers from Canada.) I told his teacher this, and she said that it didn't matter; she was just happy the kid was reading.

I cannot pass a bookstore without having a peek in. When we were in Italy, I kept going into bookstores there— in the train stations, at the airport, as we passed them on the street. If they had a fiber section, I'd look for books that had some new ideas. Sadly, the selection was limited. Finally, Brian said, "I don't understand why you insist on going into Italian bookstores, you can't *read* any of the books."

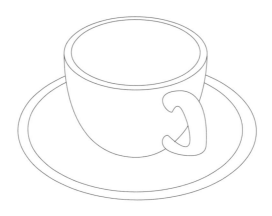

Say It with Fabric

Some people like flowers for Valentine's Day or Mother's Day. Not me; I'm allergic. Sneezing my way through a holiday does not appeal to me. Luckily, Brian (when he remembers) is a very romantic guy, and over the years, he's picked out some very nice quilt-related presents.

When we were first married, in college, we went to the fabric store in downtown West Lafayette to buy fabric that I would use to make myself an "interview suit." That was back in the days when I sewed all of my clothes for important occasions. Brian had already witnessed the creation of many long dresses for the formal dances they had in the dorms. While I was perusing suit fabric, Brian disappeared, then came back with a wrapped package. He had picked out a pair of left-handed Gingher shears. A very sweet gift—my first pair of "good scissors"—and he must have researched it enough to know that I would be more comfortable with a lefty pair than making do with normal ones.

Later on, Brian was in charge of the boy scouts' Pinewood Derby and got my scissors engraved with my name when he took the trophies in to be engraved. My name even matched the font of the Gingher logo. He thought it would make it easier to find my shears if I put them down during a workshop.

My Bernina was my fifteenth wedding anniversary present. For several years after that, Brian bought accessory feet to mark other occasions, including the anniversary of our first date. Is that not romantic?

At some point I wanted a sewing machine cabinet. They seemed expensive, and I kept putting off buying one and tried to figure out how to build one cheaply. Before I succeeded in that, Brian bought me a lovely cabinet for Mother's Day.

The next year, I received a thread rack for embroidery machines that held about twenty spools.

He ran out of gas after that and resorted to gym bags two years in a row (neither time was I that thrilled), pearl necklaces two years in a row, and forgetting special dates altogether some years. On my forty-fifth birthday, he presented me with a gold brooch made by the son of one of my quilting friends. His work has been published many times, and I often showed Brian the pictures.

"Look how gorgeous his work is, and I know his mother! She's a quilter!" I'd exclaim. The hints got more and more obvious: "If I ever had a nice piece of jewelry, I'd like it to be something made by Aaron." Sometimes I have to almost hit Brian over the head with a hammer, but it does work on occasion.

Brian fishes, and I try to get him tackle-related presents every year too, but I had run out of ideas this year. One December, I went to a store that featured fishing electronics.

"I'm looking for a fish finder for my husband," I told the clerk. "I want to know if the newer ones have different technology than the old ones. How do these work?"

The kid waiting on me said that they work with "beams."

"Magic beams? What kind of beams? Sonar? Heat-seeking somethings?" He didn't know. He wouldn't tell me if anyone else in the store could help.

I bought Brian a leather jacket that year. This year, I tried to get some hints from him but couldn't even get a direct request. Finally, I gave up. We went to the mall, I did some shopping, for Brian, then met him in the sporting-goods store.

"I found something I think I'd like," he said.

"Ah, too bad you didn't tell me that before I spent two hundred dollars on this other stuff," I answered.

"Well, that's okay. I can wait."

No, I figured if he was going to request something specific after twenty-eight years of not giving me a clue, this was a good time to listen and buy. I got him the underwater fish camera.

It is a camera that looks like a fish on a cable so the other fish don't know that it's a camera—in case fish are smart enough to recognize electronics. ("Look, Bernie, it's the 2008 XPS3000, I almost mistook it for a mackerel.") The camera that looks like a fish, sorta, has an infrared light ringing its mouth that works underwater. A little TV sits in the boat, or on the ice if you are an ice fisherman, and you can see all the little fish under the water. The fish camera (that looks like a fish) amused us all day on Christmas, but so far, Brian hasn't seen any fish with it. He thinks that the fish hide out when it is cold. I think they are at the quilt shop looking for presents for their fishwives. Until they come back, I'm going to borrow the camera to look at the underside of my quilts when they are on my longarm.

The Quilting Life

CHAPTER THREE

The Color of Things

I was in Santa Clara, California, giving a lecture and teaching a quilting class. During a free afternoon, my hostess took me to "The Mothership," which is the Apple computer store located in their main building. The main draw of the store, they told me, was that it sells clothes with the Apple logo. I needed to go there, as I love all things Apple. Of course, the main thing I bought was a T-shirt that says, "I've been to the Mothership." Let's not discuss the irony of going to a place just to buy a T-shirt that announces you were there.

While we were there, we examined the rest of the store—the stuff you can actually use for computing. They had shelves showcasing the iPod nano and shuffle. If you do not know what an iPod is, please take the earliest opportunity to go to the Apple website. IPods are beautiful electronic objects, designed to hold music, in aluminum, in different colors. In the Apple store, they were lined up in rows, arranged by color.

"Aren't these beautiful?" I exclaimed. "Look at how pretty they are, all in a row like that. I *love* stuff like that."

Marie said, "Ah, that's a bit OCD." I had never thought of it that way.

I like looking at multiples of things, arranged in color order. For example, a KitchenAid mixer display, six or seven mixers, in different colors—yellow, orange, red, purple, blue, green—all in a row in a display in the store. Makes me want to buy one, even though I don't cook, let alone bake. I just want to have one of each. That's why I like boxes of crayons so much. For five or six dollars, you can have a box of 120 crayons, each a different color, and yet all the same shape. You can take them out of the box and line them up in rows and columns, in color order.

When my kids were in grade school, they needed to have their names on all of their school supplies, including each and every pencil, crayon, and piece of chalk. I never did figure out how to label the chalk properly, but the crayons were easy. I used mailing labels, printed out the name six times on each label, and trimmed them to have 180 names per page. Enough for that huge box of crayons as well as the pencils and other stuff.

Actually, the kids didn't need boxes of 120 crayons for school. I think they needed the box of sixteen. Maybe the set of twenty-four. Definitely not even the box of sixty-four. It was me who chose to overload their desks with crayons. I couldn't help it. The stores always had big boxes of crayons on sale every fall; they were so cheap it made no sense to pay extra to get the smaller box. And that would have deprived me of the time spent with Sam putting labels, one at a time, on each crayon. I also took the time to rearrange them in color order. While I was doing that, I wondered how Crayola decided where to put each crayon in the box—their arrangement made no sense to me. Maybe they didn't actually *care*.

Maybe having things in color order is something peculiar to me, like I think ironing bed sheets is an odd habit.

Once, my mother got a new dining set, each chair a different color—yellow, orange, red, purple, blue, and green. I didn't much like the set, but I arranged the chairs in color order around the glass table and called it good. She watched wordlessly, I'm sure wondering what I was up to.

I used to keep all my threads on a wall rack, in color order of course, separated by type. Having them in order helped me see how much thread I really had. An abundance of thread was very comforting to me; I don't know why. I can tell you that when I got so much thread collected it no longer fit on racks, I moved it all into my drawer storage system, separated by manufacturer and color. And then I arranged the threads in color order in the drawer. It is completely beside the fact that when I open the drawer the spools roll around and jumble up my careful arrangement.

I sort my purchased fabrics out by color too, for the most part. I do have piles for special fabrics collected in different countries, or received as gifts. The majority are separated out into containers by color and then arranged in the containers by value, light to dark.

My dyed fabrics sit on shelves, going from yellows at the top to brown and black on the bottom. That way, it's easy to see what colors I need to dye more of (that's the excuse I use). But I know that just having the fabric folded neatly on the bookshelf isn't satisfactory; the stacks must be in a logical order or else, as far as I am concerned, they are still messy and might as well be thrown in piles on the floor. My shoebox full of scraps is in color order too.

Not everything I own is in color order. I keep my books in order generally by subject and author. Although I will admit I have thought about arranging them by jacket colors, but it would be impossible to find a particular title unless I had the covers all memorized.

When I was a little girl and I lived with my grandmother, she had a box of pearl buttons made to go onto knitted sweaters. All of the buttons were the same shape and size—shiny half spheres—with the button shank on the flat side. I used to dump them out on the carpet and run my fingers through them, then sort them into piles of different colors. When I got done, I dumped them back into the little box. Perhaps that is where this all got started. Maybe a therapist would tell me that this all goes back to a time when I felt secure—living with my grandmother and having an abundance of sweater buttons.

I also buy Fiesta dishes. My excuse is that they come in lots of colors, you aren't expected to set a table with just one hue, and I break a lot of plates. I can buy new place settings every so often, in a new color, and they all go well together. The first year, I bought five place settings in turquoise and five in deep purple. (They were having a sale on Amazon). The second year, I bought five of yellow and five of red, because I needed warm colors to complement the turquoise and purple. I forgot to see if I had broken any of the earlier collection. Since I had not, they didn't all fit on the shelves.

And since I don't like to entertain, having twenty sets of plates is just silly. Or is it? Don't you think tomato soup in a yellow bowl sitting next to macaroni and cheese on a purple plate sounds beautiful? I mean, delicious? The plates also look marvelous stacked in the cabinets, in alternating colors. I will not mention the times I load the dishwasher in alternating plate colors.

This color arranging could be an attempt to get some order in my life. Don't worry, I don't have obsessive-compulsive disorder. My entire house is not arranged in color order. Just my threads, my beads, my fabric, my yarn, my plates. . . . The whole rest of the house is a free-for-all.

I Love Lime

When I was in college, there was this girl in my dorm who loved purple. It wasn't a very popular color then. Her dorm room was completely purple: purple bedspread purple rug, purple curtains . . . I think she covered the walls with purple sheets too. I don't know what her roommate thought, but I thought she was a little odd.

I seem to be obsessed with lime green. I haven't banned other colors from my house, but I am easily amused by anything in lime green. When Saab came out with a lime green convertible, I was in love but not in a position to buy one, so I settled for a spring jacket in the same shade. I was in a state of bliss when one of my students showed up for class one day with that very car and suggested we go to dinner with the top down, and I could wear my jacket. I've been collecting things in lime for about a decade. I keep thinking the color is a fad and will disappear, but it shows up year after year—it just changes a teeny bit, and all the stuff still goes together.

As quilters, perhaps we are all obsessed with color. It would be one explanation of why we collect all that fabric. However, this color obsession can invade one's everyday life if one is not careful. Here is a quiz you can take to see if the problem is getting out of control:

1. Do you regularly check the KitchenAid website to see what colors their mixer comes in, desperately hoping that your personal favorite might be next? 5 points if you do, 50 points if you think this is a good excuse to buy a computer and start web surfing.

2. Have you ever walked into a department store and thought it was a good idea to buy a KitchenAid toaster, blender, mixer, and can opener all in different colors so you can line them up on your kitchen counter in "rainbow" order? Zero points for a "no," 5 points if it's "no" but you can see the logic in this, 10 points if you have done it, and an extra 50 points if you don't even cook.

3. Do you keep buying a particular kitchen tool, such as a colander, because you like them in (for example) lime green, but you rarely make spaghetti? 20 points for a yes.

4. I painted my son's room lime green when I turned it into a guest room. I'm thinking of keeping my colanders on a shelf in his room, because they'd look spiffy. A quilter friend suggested it, because she said it didn't matter where the colanders lived if they never got used anyway. If this argument makes sense to you, add 10 points to your score.

5. I bought a green iPod shuffle within ten minutes of them showing up on the Apple website. I had it engraved "Goddess of the Last Minute." When my daughter was visiting from college, I showed it to her

and told her that her father asked why I had bought it. "Did you tell him it was lime green? What other excuse do you need?" she replied. I still can't decide if she was in agreement with me or teasing me. So the question is, have you bought electronics just because they came in your favorite color? 10 points for yes, 20 points if you have no clue how to use it but bought it anyway.

6. Do your children tease you about buying things in that color? 10 points if yes, 20 if they have inherited this trait and try to get you to give your stuff to them.

7. Have you collected *every* paint chip at the paint store just so you can fondle the stack of color? 10 points if yes, 20 points if you decided it was better to just buy the color fan, 30 points if you own more than one version of the color fan.

8. What is the biggest box of crayons you own? 10 points for the sixty-four pack, 20 points for over one hundred. No points if you don't understand why an adult still needs a box of crayons. 100 points if you bought an entire box of sixty-four crayons in *one* color and you aren't a first grade teacher, because that's just weird.

You'll have to figure out the scoring for yourself—I'm too busy making a list of all the dye supplies I need to get that perfect lime green.

Do Irons Need a Vacation?

Irons, both steam and dry, are a hot topic of discussion amongst quilters on the internet. Compared to sewing machines, they are relatively cheap—which is good, because we seem to replace them often. We have either broken our last one or heard about a new one that has magical properties.

Without getting out of my chair, I can count five regular-sized irons in my studio: two of them aren't currently working; one connects to a steam tank through a hose; another is cordless, sitting on a base to recharge; and one is on my ironing table, ready to press something. Oh wait, here's another iron I forgot about. It's the twin to one of the broken irons. I found them on clearance at a department store when I was shopping for shoes. I bought both, thinking it would be good to have one ready for when my current one died, and Brian is always asking for a decent iron. He got to use his for about two weeks until I took it to our condo in the city to use there. Its twin died a few months ago, and I forgot I still had the spare—that's when I bought the one on a hose.

The one on the hose gives off a lot of steam, but it also takes a long time to heat up. It seemed like a good idea at the time, but I keep forgetting to fire it up right when I start quilting.

The cordless one is good if I have to fuse something on my working wall. Also, it has a titanium plate that fusible webbing won't stick to . . . unless I am in front of twenty people demonstrating how well the iron sheds fusible. I don't do that demonstration at the beginning of a class anymore because once I spent the next half hour trying to clean the goop off the iron.

Some irons shut off automatically. This is good if you are the type of person who pulls your car out of the garage and then wonders if you left the iron on. I am that kind of person. My friend Lynne did leave town with her iron on once. She called me, told me she was pretty sure it was still on, and would I go to her house and turn it off? Of course I would; she'd do it for me. Lynne told me the combination to her garage so I could get in. Indeed, she had left her iron on. It was very hot. I unplugged it and waited a while for it to cool. And waited a while longer. When I was completely bored, the iron was still hot. I wrapped it in a towel and took it home with me, convinced it was possessed. When I called Lynne to tell her I had her iron at my house, she said she figured I would do that. I still wonder why she said that—maybe she knew I'd worry until I was certain the surface was stone cold and could do no harm.

By the way, I did leave one of my own irons on overnight once. Nothing bad happened, but I wouldn't want to take that chance again. So now I use the kind that shuts itself off. When I'm not using the one with the long hose. Or the cordless one.

I never throw out my broken irons right away. For some reason I don't understand, an iron under normal use by a quilter will one day, without warning, simply refuse to heat up. After checking it several times, I set it aside for a little vacation and go out and get a new iron. When the new iron poops out, I go back to the old iron and see if it has rested enough to start working again. Quite often it does. Sometimes it needs another year; sometimes it will never work again. After three years, I will throw a broken iron out. In the meantime, I do accumulate a bunch of broken irons. I still had them out during an iron replacement session when Samantha asked if I had an iron she could take back to college with her. She was puzzled when I suggested she just go buy a new one, as none of the ones on my ironing table were working.

My first good iron was a present from Brian for Mother's Day. The kids were babies; we were broke at the time. Brian asked a quilter friend of mine what a good present would be, and she told him a good iron would be great. He bought an expensive Rowenta. (Well, at the time it was sixty dollars, and it felt expensive.) When I opened the box, I thought Brian wanted me to start pressing his shirts. Au contraire, it was just for quilting. In fact, no matter how broke we've been, Brian's shirts that needed pressing have always gone to the cleaner, because they have a special press. (And he has always ironed his own pants.) Even though, I just remembered, I also have one of those presses. It takes too much wattage to use in my studio though, and I'm afraid of it. It opens like a clamshell and has a large surface I could burn my arms on. I need to get some oven mitts to use with it.

If we leave the category of full-sized irons, we enter the realm of small irons. Those range from a little metal triangle on the tip of what once was a soldering iron to a larger iron originally made for sealing plastics. And then, my favorite, these little toy irons that have been the rage for the last few years. They are cheap—between five and ten dollars—and come in cute colors. They look just like a regular steam iron but in miniature, and whenever I use one I feel like I should be standing in one of those plastic kitchens they make for toddlers.

Quilters will also tell you many different ways to clean an iron. One technique is to iron on a fabric-softener dryer sheet. The softener in the sheet heats up accumulated goop and it wipes off the iron. This works well if the iron isn't too far gone. As a fuser, this rarely works for me, as my irons are often well past goopy. I swear by one brand and one brand only: Faultless Hot Iron Cleaner. There is another major brand that doesn't work when the goop is hardened. I know this because I used a whole tube of Brand B on an iron once when I couldn't find the Faultless anywhere. I also tried alcohol, lighter fluid, and dry-cleaning solution. I'm lucky I didn't set the house on fire. I also didn't get a clean iron. Now I keep an extra tube of Faultless around the house. You put it on a piece of toweling, heat up the iron, and iron like crazy into the towel. It helps to put the towel on the edge of a table, to add extra friction.

I'd love to chat about irons some more, but I am noticing that my last resurrected iron has a very goopy surface.

The Machine's the Thing

Here's something I've learned about quilting over twenty years: The quality of your tools and materials affects the joy you derive from quilting and the quality of your final product. Yes, I'm sure beautiful quilts have been made from cheap fabrics, using inexpensive sewing machines. However, it's so much nicer to create your vision without having to fight with your tools.

Sometimes I forget this, until I try a new craft and suddenly realize the wisdom of using good tools and materials.

My friend Kathleen and I took a jewelry class, using torches, metal saws, and harsh chemicals. I didn't enjoy myself as much as I thought I would. The jewelry I was making seemed clunky, and I didn't like the tools. I couldn't cut neat lines, and I was always melting my work with the torches. In order to make a simple hammered copper bracelet, we were told to hammer for a while, then anneal the metal with the torch—hammer, anneal, hammer, anneal, etc. It seemed like a lot of work for a bracelet I could buy in a department store for about fifteen dollars. I resorted to what I call "The Princess Method" of jewelry making: I bought a bracelet from another student and talked Kathleen into doing all the torching for me. I still enjoyed the class—

it got me out of the house twice a week, I got to spend a few hours with Kathleen, and it was a good excuse to buy a lot of jewelry books—but I was disappointed that I hadn't been able to motivate myself to actually make anything. Then it dawned on me that we were using cheap metals (copper and brass) and cheap tools that didn't cut or burn very well. The process wasn't aesthetically pleasing. I bought a piece of silver for about fifteen dollars and better saw blades and was much happier. Kathleen busied herself buying good torches and other metalworking tools, and when I can get over my fear of setting her house on fire, I bet I'll enjoy taking her up on her offer to make use of it.

I'm sure one of the reasons I prefer quilting to jewelry making has to do with the properties of the materials—soft fabric versus hard metal—but the lesson I learned with the jewelry drove home a lesson I thought I had learned in my long pursuit of quilting: Use the good stuff. It's worth it.

I LEARNED TO SEW ON A WHITE MACHINE built sometime after the turn of the last century. It went forwards and backwards. That was it. I used it to sew some clothes in elementary school. My mother threw it out (long story), and later in high school I got another machine after trying to sew clothes by hand for several years. I took that machine to college and sewed dresses for dances. I was one of the few students on my dorm floor majoring in a mostly male degree program—engineering—but was the only woman who had brought a sewing machine to school with me.

Later, I moved up (I thought) to an inexpensive Singer—mostly plastic, and mostly junk. I tried to free-motion quilt with it but gave up after breaking an entire pack of needles in one sitting. Finally, when we had a thousand dollars left in our bank account, after buying our house, I bought a used Pfaff and learned how to free-motion quilt. The Pfaff had been a top-of-the-line model, traded in after a year by someone moving up to a newer machine herself. I got rid of the plastic Singer and the old Signature that went to college with me, but I still had the Pfaff until I sent it along with my daughter to college.

Sewing machines are so amazing today: They can talk to your computer, embroider fancy designs, connect to the internet, and probably cook dinner. My main sewing machine use is limited to sewing on borders, free-motion machine quilting, and decoratively stitching on the binding. The truth is that if my machine only moved the needle up and down and stitched in a straight line and maybe one or two decorative stitches, I would be fine. *However*, there are a few features that I find really helpful when free-motion quilting. If you are looking for a new machine, consider the following:

Needle stop up/down

What it does: Lets you decide if the needle will be in the up or down position when you stop stitching. Usually the default is needle up; if you'd rather have the needle always stop down, you press a button.

Why you need it: I keep my machines set for needle down when I am free-motion quilting. When I stop stitching, the needle sinks into the quilt exactly where I stopped and keeps it from moving several inches. The needle then holds the quilt in place if I want to pivot it a bit or, more commonly, move my hands to a more comfortable position.

Knee Lift

What it does: On machines with this feature, there is usually a lever that you push with your right knee. When activated, it simultaneously raises the presser foot and drops the needle thread tension. This is the same function that the lever on the back of the machine behind the needle usually serves.

Why you need it: On a machine without the knee lift, you have to remember to go back and release the lever before you start stitching again. Sometimes you'll forget and get a thread nest on the back of your quilt. Very annoying. With the knee lift, you just stop pressing against the knee lift, the foot drops down, the upper tension is re-engaged, and off you go.

On some machines, the knee lift raises the presser foot higher than the manual lever. This makes changing presser feet a very easy task. You just lean on the knee lift, pop off the old foot, and pop on the new. If you use a walking foot and have had a hard time installing it, try it using the knee lift; it may be easier for you.

The knee lift makes it so much easier to reposition your hands on the quilt when free motioning. You can rearrange your hands and move your knee in one smooth motion.

If you chain-piece your quilts, you can use the knee lift to raise the pressure foot up, slide the new piece under the foot, against the needle (which you have set up to stop in the down position), and then step on the pedal and keep sewing.

It is much faster to slide the work from the machine when you can raise the knee lift and remove the thread tension in the same step.

I have become so accustomed to using the knee lift that I won't use a machine without it. When I'm teaching, I sit down at a student's machine to demonstrate. The first thing I do is put the knee lift in if they weren't using it. Otherwise I keep moving my right leg against air, wondering why the presser foot isn't lifting. Most brands have this feature now, and I think it's worth spending the money to get it.

Speed

Stitches per minute: Top-of-the-line machines often run faster than other models in the line, and there are also moderately priced machines that run faster than regular machines. I consider a machine that has at least 900 stitches per minute a necessity, and even faster is better. Some domestic machines run as fast as 1,500. It's not that I'm in a terrible hurry; I just have a hard time slowing down to "keep up" with a slow machine. During free-motion quilting, the feed dogs are dropped; you are regulating the stitch length by how fast you move the quilt versus how fast the machine is making a stitch. If you are moving the quilt too quickly, you will get long, uneven stitches. Although one of the first things I tell students is *not* to run the machine at full speed to avoid feeling rushed, I find that I do run most machines with the pedal all the way down, and if the machine is too slow, my stitching suffers.

Smooth speed regulation: It is possible to have the machine run too fast. I have a machine that runs at 1,500 stitches per minute at top speed. This is just too fast for me. However, the pedal isn't sensitive enough for me to easily find a consistent speed and stick with it. Luckily I found a speed control that fits on the cable between the pedal and the machine and has a dial that controls the top speed.

Adjustable tension on the bobbin case

What it does: I often need to reduce the tension on the needle thread to avoid thread shredding when using special threads such as rayon, polyester, or metallic embroidery threads. When you reduce the needle tension it is necessary to also reduce the bobbin tension in order to keep the tensions balanced. Tension that is unbalanced, with the needle tension tighter than the bobbin, will result in poorly formed stitches that look like eyelashes on the front of the quilt. When the bobbin tension is tighter than the needle tension, the eyelashes appear on the back of the quilt.

Some bobbin cases have a spring or a tongue that you put the bobbin thread through when embroidering, satin stitching, or (the manufacturer will tell you) free-motion quilting. These are stitches that will normally pull the bobbin thread to the top of the work. The tongues and springs in effect *raise* the bobbin tension, keeping the bobbin thread on the back of the work. However, raising the tensions can cause the thread to shred due to more friction as it goes through the needle, so I prefer to lower both the top and bobbin tension instead.

Sewing-machine dealers will sometimes tell their customers not to mess with the bobbin tension; my guess is because many sewers don't know how to adjust the tension back to perfection for normal stitching. I am very good at adjusting my bobbin tension, but to make life easier, I keep a second bobbin case adjusted to the perfect tension for free-motion quilting and leave the original bobbin case alone. On my machines that have an extra bobbin specifically for embroidery, I leave that one alone too and use my "special" bobbin case. I marked the latch on the case with a thin line of nail polish and scratched an "L" in it, for Lower. Someone told me once that machine dealers don't like their customers using nail polish on their bobbin cases because the polish can come off in the machine and cause problems; however, I have a bobbin case that is ten years old and still going strong. An extra bobbin case is the first purchase I make for every new machine. I won't buy a machine that doesn't have a removable bobbin case.

Extended head length
What it does: There are now many home sewing machines on the market that have a longer sewing head. The extended length of the head makes it easier to get your quilt into the machine. If you really want a lot of room, you can invest in a longarm machine, but that's a whole 'nother animal.

Bobbin thread cutter

What it does: Some machines have a button you can press to cut the bobbin thread automatically. I used to avoid using the cutter, because it still leaves about a quarter-inch tail on the back of the quilt and I can never find them all when it's time to trim the threads. However, a longarm dealer taught me a trick: stop stitching, move the quilt a few inches, and *then* press the button. This leaves a tail on the back that is several inches long. Pull this tail to the front of the quilt by tugging on the needle thread.

Cabinets

I used to think that having a sewing machine cabinet was a luxury. However, after dealing with machines sitting on top of a table, I highly recommend that every machine be kept in a sturdy cabinet. It is essential to support the entire quilt on the same horizontal surface when free-motion quilting. If some of the quilt is hanging off the edge of the stitching surface, the quilt will pull against the needle, making it easier to break the needle and harder to stitch. I keep my machines in cabinets, lowered so that the machine bed is level with the cabinet surface. You can buy an extension table for your machine, but I feel it is better to have the whole top of the cabinet to work with. I have my cabinets set up next to a dining table so that the entire quilt can be supported at once.

Lowering the height of the sewing bed when using a cabinet will also help you ergonomically; your shoulders won't get all hunched up and start hurting.

Cabinets are also more stable than many tables. I find it extremely annoying when a machine is bouncing around on a table; my eyes get tired quickly.

Look at the mechanism for lowering the sewing machine in a cabinet. I find an "airlift" to be the most desirable method of raising and lowering the machine. I have a cabinet that doesn't have this; to raise and lower the machine you tilt the supporting shelf and move it around. It's a lot of work. I found that I was avoiding using the embroidery module of my machine just because I didn't want to hassle with lifting the machine up. The airlift will easily raise the machine above the cabinet surface to install the embroidery module, and it will lower it beneath the cabinet surface with just a push.

Basic sewing tables can be had for under a hundred dollars. On the other end of the spectrum, there is a cabinet that has built-in cup holders and programmable buttons to raise the entire surface to your perfect height. I think it costs more than my last sewing machine.

TALK TO OTHER QUILTERS to find out what brand of sewing machine they recommend—everyone has at least one favorite—and get the best machine your budget will accommodate. Consider that your first machine probably won't be your last, and like many quilters, you might end up with a collection of machines. Talk to your local dealer too; buying from a bricks-and-mortar vendor is worth a higher price when you need service or lessons, and they often have a good selection of used machines.

You'll Have to Pry These Scissors from My Cold, Dead Hands

You can never have a pair of scissors that is too sharp, nor can you have too many pairs. If you are like me, your favorite pair is guarded carefully from marauding family members who will try to cut electrical wire with your favorite sewing shears. I trained my kids early. I remember Josh telling his baby sister to keep away from a pair, warning her that they were sharp. I think I got carried away because when Josh was in kindergarten his teacher told me he was the only kid who was afraid of scissors.

The reverence for a good cut runs deep. I still have my grandmother's sewing scissors, and they still work well. However, I also have a huge collection of newer scissors and shears in all sizes and types: little tiny baby nail scissors that I can take along on a plane trip, giant shears to cut upholstery, and in between at least a hundred pairs in various blade configurations. I have a pair that lives in a little silver pocket, hanging on a chain around my neck; machine-embroidery models that hang from knotted shoelaces on a wall storage unit next to my sewing machine; left-handed versions of all sizes and types.

I have a teeny tiny pair, very sharp, bought at a hand-appliqué workshop, from the teacher. Not that I ever do hand appliqué, but when I want to start, I'm ready with the proper equipment.

Once, I bought thirty pairs in an eBay auction. They had been confiscated at airport security at the Northwest airlines terminal in Minneapolis. Most of them have dull blades; I plan to put them in a shadow box and hang them on a wall as art.

I keep my scissors sorted into plastic drawers in my "wall o' drawers." The larger shears are stored in a cutlery divider in a drawer marked "scissors." The smaller, thrown into another drawer marked "smaller scissors," and even more in another drawer marked "more scissors."

I have many duplicates of the models that I use most often. I keep them scattered around the house, to avoid having to stop what I'm doing and look for a pair. I use kitchen scissors to cut up chicken breasts and green onions, and to trim crusts off sandwiches.

I travel with several pairs in my teaching suitcase. I carry only cheap scissors on airplanes anymore. I had a nice pair of blunt-tipped school scissors and lost them on a train in New Zealand. I was beading, the train went around a bend, my beads flew around, and the scissors fell on the floor. I was so busy corralling loose beads I forgot to grab the scissors. I realized they were gone two days later at the Wellington airport when they didn't show up on the x-ray machine. Here's a hint for flying with scissors: don't leave them in your carry-on, even if they are the proper size and configuration for flying. Take them out and hand them to the security person for hand inspection. You'll get through security faster, and they won't have to root through all your stuff to find them.

It's worth carrying a cheap pair that you don't mind giving up. Brian and I flew together one day, and he was wearing a new sports jacket. He had remembered to cut the threads that held his pockets closed but failed to notice a thread that held the vent flaps closed. I didn't have anything sharp with me, so I handed Brian a plastic knife we got at breakfast and told him to saw the threads apart.

The construction of my own quilts involves ironing paper-backed fusible webbing onto fabric and then cutting elaborate shapes out of the fabric/paper sandwich. Since paper dulls scissor blades, I have special pairs set aside for this purpose. I don't use cheap ones; I have one model designated for just cutting the paper-backed webbing, another model set aside for cutting the fabric/paper sandwich. My current set has lasted a few years. When they dull, I'll have them sharpened or buy another set on sale. I find the process of cutting out the designs with a good pair of scissors to be very satisfying.

I can't be the only quilter with a scissors obsession. I'm sure the majority of quilters have this same quirk—that would explain all the manufacturers that have commemorative sets every year. Those make great gifts. Recently, I was talking to my daughter's boyfriend. His mother quilts, and I suggested that he consider getting some for his mom for

Mother's Day this year. If he doesn't, I might send her the pair I got as a gift at a quilt show last year (they were normal shears, and I'm left handed). I'm sure she can always use another pair.

Working on Workmanship

There are art quilters out there who think that workmanship doesn't matter in an art quilt. Their position is that in art quilts, design trumps everything.

I will agree that in art quilts, design is extremely important. (I could also argue that many art quilts don't seem to have much design either—a lot of them look like stuff thrown at the background and stitched in place wherever they fell, but that's another topic.)

Please keep in mind that I don't judge quilts very often and have no formal training in quilt judging; I just like to look at quilts. What I say here is totally unrepresentative of any quilt show judging practices.

Personally, I don't like looking at quilts that have poor craftsmanship. Hanging threads, jerky free-motion quilting, poor color choices, and huge knots on the back of the quilt all distract me from enjoying the design. When I meet a friend for lunch, I take a shower, put on clean clothes that are appropriate for the occasion, and get there on time. To me, looking at a poorly put together quilt in a show is like having a friend who shows up for lunch an hour late in ripped-up clothes and dirty hair. Cleaning up your quilt is a sign of respect for the viewer.

I don't expect perfect workmanship on every quilt I look at; in fact, I can't deliver that myself. If every quilt of mine had to be perfect before it left the house, I'd still be working on my first one. And none of my fused quilts would ever see the light of day because I get some fraying on the edges. And if you put a gun to my head and threatened to shoot if I did another fused binding, I'd tell you to pull the trigger now. But quilters can make a reasonable attempt at fine craftsmanship, surely at least on the elements they can control, and hope they will be forgiven for their flaws.

Burying the tail ends of your quilting threads is a simple matter, it just takes time. One quilt I made last year had hundreds of thread ends. The border section took three hours to quilt and six hours to bury all the thread ends. I used to bury thread for about half an hour, then lose patience and just start clipping the threads. Over the year, some of those ends worked themselves loose. It embarrasses me when I start noticing that the stitching is coming out, especially when I see it midsentence when I am pointing something else out to a student. I do use it as a teaching moment and tell them this is why I now bury my threads. Very often I look at my own quilts and find some weird thing I wish I could improve. I've never looked at one of my quilts and thought to myself that I wasted my time by doing that one part exactly right.

Some quilt artists argue that the back of the quilt shouldn't matter; they say that no one looks at the back of a painting, why should they look at the back of the quilt? First of all, most paintings are hung in such a way that you can't see the back of it without pulling it off the wall. (Something that the gallery or museum curator might not appreciate.) For all I know, it might be expected that paintings are finished well on the back. Obviously sculptures are finished well on all sides. When I took a jewelry class at the community college, the instructor emphasized good workmanship on the back, too, as she said that most buyers would want to turn the piece over and examine the back. It is very easy to examine the back of a quilt; you simply lift the corner up or ask the nice white-gloved quilt-show angel to do that for you. Making sure the back of your quilt is neat is like always wearing clean underwear in case you get hit by a car. But in the case of a quilt, it doesn't take a major calamity for someone to want to see the back of it, and having threads hanging off all over the place is like wearing underpants with holes in them.

If the quilt is hanging in a quilt show that is part of a contest, it is likely that it will be judged by a team, and at least one member will have been trained to judge quilts using the traditional standards of quilt-show judging. They don't even have to have made a quilt. Judging a quilt can be very subjective: one judge will love your color scheme, another hate it. One will get the message in your political quilt and agree with you, another might hate what you have to say, and a third might not even understand that there is a message. You can't count on them getting the artistic value of the quilt, because certified judges aren't required to have art training. When the subjective values of a quilt are murky, the judges will fall back on objective things like the workmanship.

What one quilter thinks is artistry, another thinks is sloppiness. Take free-motion quilting stitch length. Quilt show judges seem to comment on this all the time, and it isn't just limited to traditional judges. I judged once with an art quilter who insisted a quilt had uneven stitching, and that really bothered her. Personally, I feel that varying quilting stitches are a sign that a human being did the quilting, as opposed to a machine. A hand holding a pencil is going to make lines that vary in thickness, as opposed to a graphic design printed out on a computer. However, I like to see that a quilter is making an attempt to have even stitches.

When I am working on my own quilts, I try to remember the words of a professor who taught a Basic Color and Design class I took at the community college: "Straight lines should be straight and curved lines should be smooth." While I don't take that literally, I do think of it as an admonition to mean what you do. Don't be sloppy because you are lazy; be sloppy if it makes your point. But make sure that the viewer *knows* you are making that point.

Now that I have said all that, please don't let my comments keep you from making quilts because you don't think they will measure up. It took me a few years to get started, because I thought that if I couldn't make the points match, everyone would think it was a terrible quilt. That is not true, and people have written books about making quilts that intentionally have points that don't come near each other. It took a while before I learned tricks to make my points match, and then it was no longer something I even thought about. I still can't make all my points match, and I don't care—I just do fused appliqué instead. Can't do a regular binding, so I do a fused binding. And I'll keep trying to make my workman-ship better.

Clutter Control

My house is cluttered. My quilting stuff is everywhere. When I was doing my taxes, I deducted my studio as a home office. It is completely given over to quilting; you *can't* do anything else in there. The truth is that if the IRS had come over during the month of April, they probably would have said, "Just deduct the whole house. You are obviously using every room for your business."

My house has always been cluttered, except for the years when both kids were toddlers and putting everything in their mouths and, frankly, we were too broke to have anything to clutter up the house. My floors were clean then too, because I was constantly mopping up spills. We had some friends over one day; I was sitting on the wood floor, eating nuts out of a bowl. I knocked the bowl over and kept eating the nuts. I'm sure my friend thought I was a pig, but at that point, the floor was the cleanest surface in the house.

As the babies got older, the clutter increased. We seem to collect stuff in this family. My son, Josh, cleaned out his closet and brought some stuff down to the basement. It was a laundry basket full of toys.

"Do we really need to keep this toy wrestling ring?" I asked.

"Yes!"

I think the only reason he was able to clean up was the comforting belief that I wouldn't throw it out. He is about to move out permanently, and I still haven't thrown his toys out, and I won't. I promised Josh that I wouldn't toss anything unless he gives me specific permission. In turn, he has promised to clean out as much as possible this summer when he comes home to visit.

Anyway, clutter has been an issue for me. The neighbors' houses seem very clean, maybe because I really only see them when they've cleaned up for a party. My two closest friends seem to have very clean houses. Whenever they come over, I have the impulse to clean up clutter during their visit, as I suddenly see it in their eyes. I'm trying to get myself to stop doing this. They've been my friends a long time, and they know what I'm like. Why try to change their opinion now?

Quilting friends are the best kind. I hate to generalize, but I have to be honest and say that most of the ones I meet will admit to having cluttered homes. I will say, though, that when I travel to teach and stay at a quilter's home, the houses are *always* nice and clean—no clutter. I will assume either that they clean up beforehand or that the guild only lets the one or two neatniks in the group host visiting teachers. I've also noticed that most of these quilters no longer have children living at home.

My son's new girlfriend was coming for a visit during a college break, so my husband started cleaning the house, to make a good impression. We told Josh this, and he said,

"It's okay, her mother is a quilter." Ah. I still let Brian do his thing. Why waste an opportunity for a clean house done by someone else?

I used to think I was dysfunctional, then I read *Organizing for the Creative Person: Right-Brain Styles for Conquering Clutter, Mastering Time, and Reaching Your Goals* by Dorothy Lehmkuhl and Dolores Cotter Lamping. Turns out, I am not dysfunctional, I am not psychologically unbalanced, I am right-brained. I *need* to see my stuff. This book helped me organize some; I highly recommend it. If you don't end up with a cleaner house, at least you'll feel better about yourself and your clutter.

I found another book, *Organizing from the Inside Out: The Foolproof System For Organizing Your Home, Your Office and Your Life* by Julie Morgenstern. The idea is to store things neatly where they end up. It works for some things, but not for our shoe problem. We seem to collect shoes in our family. Sam must have sixty pairs; she buys about a pair a week, and they all end up in front of the hall closet. I have tried various ways of storing her shoes, including getting nice shoe racks, begging her to take her shoes up to her room, and putting them in paper bags. They all end up in the front hallway, in a big pile. It doesn't help that my shoes seem to accumulate under the computer desk in the family room. My husband's shoes accumulate in front of my kitchen chair, until I trip over them and deposit them on top of Sam's shoe collection. My son has only about ten pairs of shoes, but he has giant feet, so they take up a lot of space. We can tell the kids have friends over when we come home and can't get in the front door because of the big mound of giant shoes.

Further reading of *Organizing from the Inside Out* inspired me to spend two days tearing into my kitchen cabinets and rearranging everything. This was *not* a good idea. No one could find anything and, several years later, we still haven't fully recovered from that escapade.

Emotional Design: Why We Love (or Hate) Everyday Things by Donald A. Norman is an amazing book. Halfway through the introduction, I found validation for my desperate need for an Apple Powerbook laptop computer. I had bought a laptop earlier, with the Windows XP operating system, in order to interface with my sewing machine and run the embroidery software for it. I thought maybe I'd bond with it and be able to use it to replace an older Apple laptop. I didn't bond with it. Never have. It sits all by itself, neglected on a shelf. In the meantime, I've bought two more Apple laptops, feeling guilty about neglecting that poor Windows machine. Well, Mr. Norman's book explained it all. He's a professor of computer science and psychology at Northwestern University. He even has a teapot collection, just like me! He explains that research has shown that when one is happy and contented, one can be more creative. And having a beautiful computer that you enjoy using can indeed help you be more creative. Five pages into the book, I was so excited that I wrote to him and asked him to take a look at the quilts on my website. They are all about teapots and other well-designed household items. I didn't expect him to write back, but he answered me the next day. He'd enjoyed my website. I think. Unless it was one of those "thanks for writing, your stuff is lovely, now get off my back and get some therapy" letters.

Another book I really enjoyed was *The Tipping Point: How Little Things Can Make a Big Difference* by Malcolm Gladwell. His book is about social epidemics and how they come about. It appears that my propensity to tell people what the best stuff for quilting is, and where to get it cheapest, is not an aberration; it is part of being a Maven. A maven is one of the personality types necessary to get a fad going. Mavens aren't crazy—they are actually useful! I hope you will take a look at the books I've mentioned; perhaps they can help you too.

Sizing Up a Quilt

Final exam or pop quiz? Stephen King novel or a collection of short stories? *Vanity Fair* or *People?* The size of the quilt often determines how long you'll spend making it. Unless you decide to make a fast quilt out of big squares.

I don't much like to make bed quilts. In fact, the only time I finished one was under duress when I was designing a line of quilting fabric and a magazine wanted a large quilt for the cover of their magazine. The truth is that I still didn't piece the top; a friend did that in exchange for my services—machine quilting a quilt of her choice at a later date.

I don't like making little teeny quilts either, like artist trading cards (the size of business cards), or quilted postcards, or even quilts the size of a sheet of paper. Although thinking about it, if I saved the parts I cut off when trimming my larger quilts, I'd probably have a whole bunch of them.

The true answer to the question of how big to make a quilt, for me, is "big enough." I like to make quilts to submit to national quilt shows. I need the pressure of meeting a deadline to help me focus on finishing the quilt.

Most quilt shows have several categories. Sometimes the divisions have to do with how the quilt is made (appliqué vs. piecing) or designed (traditional vs. contemporary). Usually these categories are further divided into size (small vs. large). Often the prizes for the large quilts are, accordingly, bigger than the prizes for the smaller quilts. Every once in a while, I win a ribbon—although I never expect to, or even enter a show thinking it is a done deal. But I figure if I'm going to spend the time to make the quilt, and the money to ship it to a show, I might as well make a quilt that will fit into the larger category.

If you are submitting a quilt to a show, you will have to ship it. The bigger the quilt, the more it will cost to ship, and the more you'll have to fold it—and if you want to send it in a tube, you'll have to find a long enough tube.

So, the first question I ask myself is how small "big" can be. Back in 2002, the American Quilter's Society Show in Paducah, Kentucky—one of the biggest shows in the country—required a large quilt to be at least sixty inches wide, and I want to say eighty inches long. I suspect this size is a throwback to the time when most quilts were made for beds; a queen-sized mattress is 60 x 80 inches.

I try to have a quilt ready to submit to Paducah every year, because the show is nearby, it's a big show, and it's a good goal to aim for at the end of the year, as the deadline is usually the first week in January. The quilt I was planning to enter was designed to be exactly 60 x 80 inches. I forgot that quilts shrink when you quilt them. The more you quilt, the more it will shrink. As I was binding the quilt, I stopped and measured, and the quilt was exactly 59 x 79 inches. This would not do at all. I already had another quilt I wanted to submit to the smaller category. What to do? I went to the nearby chain store and bought a few yards of thick felt, cut it into strips, and added it onto the sides of the quilt, holding it in place with a very wide binding to cover the join at the back, and I used the original binding strips as a border. As I quilted the new border, my husband came in to see what I was doing. "Since you cut it too close in the first place, don't you think you should have added five or six inches, just in case?" he asked. This is one reason I do a lot of work at night; Brian goes to sleep earlier than I do.

I did follow his advice the next time, and now I leave an extra five or six inches on each side, if I can, and then trim off the excess after quilting. I don't do complicated pieced borders, so I can get away with this. One time though, I wasn't paying close attention and trimmed a quilt to be exactly 60 x 60 inches. The problem was that the border on the left side was four inches wide and the border on the right was six inches. So far, no one has noticed that either.

One thing I do is leave the outer border larger than I want it to be, quilt it, and then trim it. If I am cutting borders lengthwise on the grain of the fabric, I often split the whole width into four strips and put the entire strip on the quilt. I also leave the whole width of the backing fabric on until I am done. I find this extra area makes a good place to test the thread tension when I am at the quilting stage.

A Quilter's Wardrobe

I was at my art-quilt critique group today, when one of the women mentioned that she loves when she has a chance to spend the day in her pajamas. Another said that would make her depressed. I said, "Staying in pajamas all day? To me, that's January." Actually, it's January, February, and March. The rest of the months too, if I can get away with it. My theory is that it is not necessary to get dressed unless one is actually going to leave the house.

One nice, sunny day, Brian was working at home, and we took a break on the front porch. The UPS truck drove up, and the guy got out and said, "Robbi! It's nice to see you dressed for a change." I had to explain my pajama theory to Brian, who wondered how close I was to the deliveryman. My theory would also explain why I find packages on the front porch without hearing the doorbell ring. I thought the bell was too quiet, but I suspect the guy just dumps the package and runs.

The act of designing a quilt does not require a formal wardrobe, or even clean hair. I stay in my pajamas and avoid taking a shower until I have to go out or need some inspiration. The running water seems to give birth to a lot of creative solutions, so I save it for when I'm stuck. Why waste

141

that gift in the morning when I'm not awake yet? I'm not a total pig; I won't leave the house without showering and dressing like an adult person. But if I have nowhere to be, I don't leave just to leave. In the winter, especially, it's silly to go out unless you have to. The streets may be icy—why risk a car accident for no apparent reason? It's cold out there, even if it hasn't snowed, and if it *has* snowed, I have to rev up the snow thrower and do the driveway before I get going. One rough winter, I announced that I had had enough; we were moving somewhere warm. Brian noted that we had agreed to stay put until the kids graduated from high school, which was half a decade away.

"Okay, I'll stay. But I'm not driving in the winter if I don't want to," I declared. "And you can't make me." After that, my husband called every day from his office asking if I had left the house today and if I wanted him to pick anything up on the way home.

It is not necessary and, in fact, seems counterproductive to get dressed to dye fabric. I do have a pile of "dye clothes." These consist of T-shirts that already have dye on them and pants with holes in them. Dark pants with holes in them aren't the best idea. You have to be able to *see* the dye on them to know they're "dye clothes" and be assured you won't wear them to the bookstore, where you'll notice a hole in the crotch, just when you are bending over to see a book on the bottom shelf, with your white underwear hanging out for everyone to see. Not that I would know anything about that.

I used to have a "dye nightgown." That was for when I felt totally lazy but wanted to dye fabric. I threw it out though, after my father-in-law was staying with us and came downstairs to have a chat while I was in the middle of a dye session. It was too hard to hold the front of the nightie closed while standing on a ladder and pouring dye. I don't want to be caught like that again.

I do get dressed if I am using the sewing machine; at least in clothes I can wear in public. One of my friends got a needle stuck in her finger and had to get dressed—painfully, avoiding catching the needle on her clothes—before she could drive to the emergency room. I do not want to tempt fate. I wear shoes when I stitch too. Would you want to put shoes on one handed? I certainly couldn't figure out how to tie the laces.

If my husband is working at home, I can stay undressed, because in an emergency situation, he'll be able to throw a robe around me as he tosses me into the car. He likes to avoid a shower until later too, but since he doesn't own any actual pajamas, he dresses in old clothes. He does wear shoes (I think it has to do with his bad feet), and it's really annoying, because he clops around the house in them. The sound bothers me. I try to deal with it though, because Brian will cook dinner on those days. And in the evening, when he's calling me to dinner, he sometimes points out that the sun has gone down and I still am dressed like an unmade bed. Which is especially sad in July.

When I do get dressed, it's still nothing to shout about. At five feet tall, I'm not model material. My favorite outfit is this big, black, linen, button-down shirt. It's loose, it's long, and for some reason I haven't figured out, it seems to be the only linen shirt I've ever owned that not only doesn't wrinkle, it doesn't shrink. I wear it as often as I can and always when flying to a booking. I say it's in case I don't have time to change before a lecture, but the truth is that I just like wearing this shirt—it's comfy, and I feel like I look good in it. The side seam is fraying though; it's getting old. I've looked for a replacement for the last two years. Can't find one. I googled the manufacturer, but no joy, as the British say. I wish I had bought five or six of these. I did find a nice brown shirt that has some of my beloved shirt's qualities, except that it is not black, and therefore not as formal. It was on sale, marked down from one hundred dollars to twenty. I bought three, because that was all they had.

I need to find a more varied wardrobe. Last month when I was flying to Ottawa, the gate agent recognized me from an earlier flight to Houston. I'm sure it was the shirt. Or maybe it was my fabulous turquoise necklace. Yeah, it was the necklace.

Addiction to Submission

I propose that entering quilt shows is addictive. I have a list of shows that I look forward to creating work for every year. If I have nothing to submit, because I didn't make enough quilts in time, I am very disappointed in myself. Last year, I even missed submitting something to the big show in Houston because all of my quilts had already been submitted to them. I was working on a quilt at the time and could have hurried up and finished it, but I wanted to take my time and produce something lovingly instead of succumbing to my habit of rushing quilts to meet a deadline.

I keep track of my quilt show appearances on my resumé and, looking at the list, I've submitted to the Houston show year after year for a long time. Twice I haven't been accepted. The ratio of acceptances to rejections is very good. Same with some other shows.

When a fellow quilt teacher who had juried that show asked if I had submitted, I had to admit that I had not. I think I felt worse than if I had submitted a quilt and not gotten in; it was a wasted opportunity. I was down in Houston for the show last year, and I was also there the last time I *did* submit something and didn't get in. I lived to tell the tale and, maybe because I was teaching, I felt better. But I missed that part of the year when they start calling people up and telling them they won something. I was very happy to have a quilt already in the works for next year.

Here are some clues that you might have an addiction to submitting quilts to quilt shows:

1. You rant about this one woman who seems to win all the ribbons.

2. You can discuss the pros and cons in great detail of every large show: which has the highest entry fees, which has the steepest return shipping fees, which has the earliest deadline in comparison to the other shows.

3. You think that the show administrators are setting their calendar to keep your quilt the longest so that no one else can have it.

4. You give up spending time with your family in December because you are too busy finishing a quilt for an early January deadline.

5. You think the show organizers of that show are plotting to keep you away from your family at Christmas.

6. You collect every cardboard carton that arrives in your house in case you can use it to ship a quilt. Here's something to think about: Your quilt will never fit in a shoebox. Throw it out.

7. The FedEx guy is trained to never leave a box on your porch in case it has a quilt in it.

8. You have a "lucky" clerk at the post office.

9. You lie to your family about how much money you spend on quilt-show entry fees.

10. You refer to all quilt shows by the city they are held in: Houston, Paducah, Harrisburg, Santa Clara, etc.

11. You stay up all night after the awards are announced for a quilt show you can't attend, hoping someone will list the ribbon-winners online. You keep going to the same internet page over and over, waiting for someone to have mercy and post the list.

Quilt-Show Rejection

One of the first quilting books I ever studied was the Quilt National catalog, back in the nineties. Quilt National is an "International Exhibition of Innovative Quilts," and it occurs every two years. It is meant to be a showcase for art quilts. When I finally got around to making art quilts, I felt that getting into QN, as I like to refer to it, would be an important affirmation of my artistic skills.

Most quilt shows have a jurying process: you send in images of your quilt (either on a CD or slides, depending on how tech savvy the organizers are) along with a check, then wait several weeks until you get an envelope with the jury results of your submission. If you are in, the envelope is usually thick, often containing mailing labels to use when you send the quilt back, a congratulatory letter, sometimes a name tag, and, in the days of slides, you'd get your slides back too. If you get rejected, the envelope usually contains merely a form letter. It's gotten so that I can feel the envelope contents on the way back from the mailbox without opening it and know if I've been accepted or not.

It took three tries to get into Quilt National. The first time I was rejected, I probably took it in stride, but the second time, not so much. I was devastated. Looking back, the quilts I submitted weren't that good. Here is what I wrote and put up on my website after that second try:

What if quilt shows offered you the chance to write your own acceptance/rejection letter? Or what if they wrote letters saying what they really *meant, instead of those nice ones that usually say how hard it was to choose just a few quilts out of all the excellent ones that were sent to them?*

Here are a few of my offerings:

‹ Your work has been accepted into our quilt show; please peel yourself off of the ceiling at your earliest convenience.

‹ Your work has been accepted into our quilt show; please follow the enclosed directions for shipping it to us. And thanks for the box of homemade cookies. The jury was impressed.

‹ Your work has not *been accepted into our quilt show; please proceed to the nearest quart of mint-chocolate-chip ice cream and dig in.*

‹ Your work is fabulous; we can't believe we didn't notice this before and have you in our quilt show every year. In the meantime, we are looking forward to receiving your current entry and possibly putting it on the cover of our book.

‹ We declined to accept your work in this year's quilt show, due to the butt-headedness of our jury. Although we could not convince them to recant, we have

decided never to have them again, and next time we will ask them what they think of your work before we invite them to jury.

• We're sorry, we cannot accept your work into our quilt show this year. In fact, we doubt we'll ever accept your work into our quilt show. Perhaps you should consider learning to operate a pottery wheel. We're keeping your slides in an effort to prevent you from inflicting your poor taste on another jury.

• We are declining your quilt entry this year. Whatever made you think we would consider a quilt using puce and chartreuse in the same quilt? We are enclosing a free coupon for a color class at your local community college.

• Puleeze! Your work looks just like (insert famous quilter's name here). Haven't you had an original idea in the last ten years? Not that (insert famous quilter's name here) has, but that's beside the point.

• We are so sorry to have declined to accept your work into this year's quilt show. Your work is so incredibly amazing, the workmanship divine, nothing else submitted can stand up to it, why the whole show would have looked shabby compared to your work. Since we do not want to hurt the rest of the artists' feelings, we have decided not to show them up by including your work.

• Dear Mrs. Eklow: Even though, technically, your husband's 1966 Oldsmobile Toronado does qualify as a quilt (three layers: metal, upholstery, and padding, held *together by bolts), we feel that the shipping costs of the traveling show would be prohibitive. We did consider using the trunk as a storage area for the rest of the show, but we can't find a garage big enough to house the car, and its reported gas mileage of five gallons to the mile makes that idea inefficient. That said, we do admire your efforts to find a way to get rid of the vehicle once and for all without hurting your husband's feelings.*

• *Dear Mrs. Robbi Joy Eklow: Unfortunately for you, we aren't taking your quilt/quilts into our show this year. Mrs. Robbi Joy Eklow, we had over 750 submittals, but we can only show 25 quilts. However we do appreciate the forty-dollar entry fee you sent; please send another fifty dollars if you'd like a ticket to the opening night. We need to cover our expenses. Mrs. Robbi Joy Eklow, your work was one of the outstanding entrees, and we're not just saying that even though this is obviously a form letter.*

• *Dear Mrs. Eklow, we can't accept your quilts into our multimedia show this year. We prefer the avant-garde work we've been showing for the past forty years and will continue to reserve our exhibition space for those artists who've shown their work for that period of time. And this year, we'd appreciate it if you'd decline to send a rebuttal letter to our rejection letter. We don't care if you think those fabric blankets of yours deserve to hang next to or in place of the lovely oil paintings of dogs playing poker.*

‣ Please return the enclosed postcard along with a check for fifty dollars to receive a ticket to the opening night reception. We know you'd like nothing better than to spend an evening fawning over the artists who did make it into our fabulous show. Drinks will start at nine o'clock; ten dollars for wine, fifteen dollars for margaritas. And we've got those cute little hot dogs floating in barbeque sauce. Three dollars.

Me again. That bit of entertainment made me feel better at the time. When I'm cranky or worried, humor goes a long way to assuage my negative feelings. I did get into Quilt National on the third try, got rejected again on the fourth and fifth tries. The sixth attempt was short circuited by the simple fact that I had nothing worthy of submittal that was brand-new work. Quilt National likes to have what I call "virgin" quilts: They haven't been seen by anyone. This is to make it more exciting for visitors to the exhibition.

Quilt Visions, The Art of the Quilt, is another exhibition in the same flavor, but they don't have the virgin-quilt requirement. I've submitted a few times in the past but haven't gotten in. This year, I had a quilt that had won two ribbons in other large shows, and I felt it was worth the attempt. One of the internet mailing groups I belong to had a post from a member whose work was accepted into the current Visions; she just found out last Friday. This morning, Brian offered to go get the mail, so I handed him the outgoing bills and said, "Bring me back my Visions acceptance." Brian, because he knows what's good for him, did bring back an envelope. A thin one. As I took it from him I said, "Ah, let's see what rejection form letter they sent this time." He asked how I knew it was a rejection—wouldn't they have sent back the slides? No slides, and they keep the CD. I opened the envelope, read the first sentence about how hard it was to pick the quilts, and immediately knew there was no chance this was an acceptance. Brian, in his unlimited need to be helpful, pointed out the sentence about how sorry they were to reject my work.

I'm good with the shows that take my work, and I do like to make the quilts I make. I have had enough validation of my talents that this current rejection won't sting as much as the earlier ones. I will admit that I immediately ripped the letter and envelope into tiny shreds and tossed it out. I am not one to save rejection letters; I know others who have quite a collection. I don't see the need to remind myself that I'm not living up to someone else's standards. If I ever forget, I have my offspring to remind me. Also, my work tends not to get accepted into the "arty type" quilt shows. Although my quilts aren't traditional, perhaps they aren't art, and that's okay.

I did sit down at the computer to find the rejection article I had written on my website and, because it had been so long since I last read it, found myself laughing again. And I'm going to make myself feel all better by doing some internet shopping. Perhaps for some knitting needles . . . there must be an "art knitting show" out there somewhere.

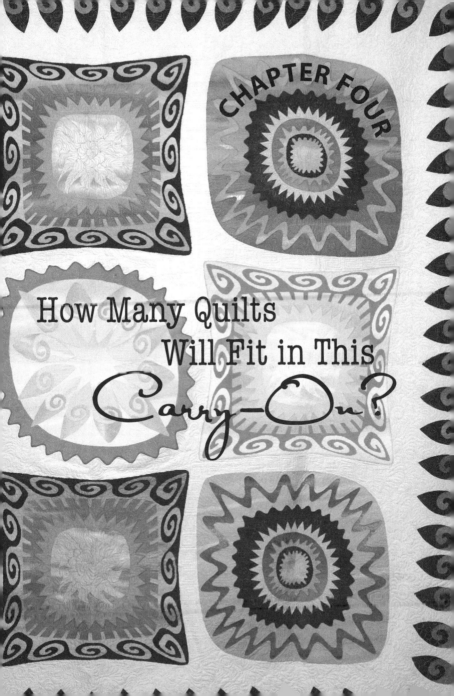

CHAPTER FOUR

How Many Quilts Will Fit in This Carry-On?

I Make the Lists

Whenever I am feeling under stress, I make a list. No, not one of those "things I'm grateful for" lists or the kind where you draw a line down a sheet of paper and put the reasons why you should do something on the left and why you shouldn't on the right. (Although, thinking back, when Brian and I decided to get married our senior year in college, we did make a list of reasons why we should get married—the kind of reasons that my parents might find good enough to foot the bill for not only the wedding but that last semester in college when we would live in married student housing.)

I usually make a list in the beginning of the day. Things I *have* to do, like mail out book or pattern orders, ship a quilt, grocery shop, or other details of life. Sometimes I'm waiting for things, like mail order deliveries, contracts, magazines, or money someone owes me.

If I have a feeling I'm forgetting something, or I'm worried I will forget something, I make the list at night, before I go to bed—then I can sleep and not worry about what I might forget. Tonight my list for tomorrow includes renewing my license plate sticker, going to the bank, buying my husband a birthday present, and looking for a pair of yellow shoes to wear to the football game this Saturday. My list for next week includes putting a sleeve on my quilt and shipping it to a show, filling out two teaching contracts, and having the car dealer figure out why my car is acting funny. Buying my husband a birthday present is going to be hard; he doesn't have any hobbies. He does like to fish, but I already discovered that he isn't missing any fishing tackle, unless I want to buy him a bass boat. I did come up with a really great idea a few months ago. I put it on a list of possible presents for him, but now I can't *find* the list. And I can't remember what is on it at all. Hopefully by Christmas the list will turn up.

One list that I have to make sure I don't lose is the list of stuff to take along when I'm teaching. I'm always worried that I'll forget something. Once when I was four hours into an eight-hour drive to a quilt show, I realized I didn't remember to check that my slide tray was in the trunk. It had been in a bag along with some other things I needed for the lecture, none of them that important, except the slides. I stopped for lunch and to check—sure enough, the bag was not there. It was in the living room. I left a message on the answering machine at home for Brian to overnight the slide tray to me. It was only Wednesday; I needed the tray for a Friday evening lecture. Brian was great about sending it, although he also sent everything else in the bag, and it was *very* expensive. The show was at a convention center with a hotel attached, and the hotel gave me a hard time about accepting a delivery. They wanted to charge me for it, and they weren't sure they would get it. I informed them that I was a guest at the hotel, I was going to lecture in front of several hundred people, and they did *not* want me to be standing there with nothing to show them, because I wouldn't be shy about blaming it on them.

Another quilt teacher, who has taught much longer than I, told me to keep a list of everything I needed to bring and check off each item as I loaded it into the car. I do that, and it works well, especially when I am still up at two o'clock in the morning before an early flight, repacking everything. I put the two suitcases, my purse, and my carry-on holding my laptop and projector near the door, checking off everything on the list. When we are pulling out of the driveway, I double check with Brian that he loaded two suitcases and one carry-on into the trunk. I have my purse clutched to my chest already.

Another technique I use to avoid forgetting something when I'm teaching is to just leave my "teaching" suitcase packed all the time. It stays in the living room, next to a box that holds items I won't be taking on that trip. I used to unpack all suitcases whenever I got home, but I found myself wasting two days looking for everything again. I was thinking about getting an armoire to keep the suitcase in; Brian suggested we just throw a cover over it and call it a coffee table.

I still forget things when I'm teaching locally. Last week I left home without the power supply to my laptop. I needed that to connect the laptop to the digital projector, in order to give my lecture. I was closer to the Apple store than to home, so I stopped and bought a new one. Now I have an extra to pack along with the digital projector. However, had I remembered to keep a list of things to bring, that would not have happened. For some reason, teaching when I can drive instead of fly makes me feel more comfortable that I won't forget something. That's not true, so I'll have to make a list of the lists to check before I leave the house.

Rant

Quilt-show season is starting up again. I can tell because it's time to buy my new pair of walking shoes. I get one pair in the fall and one in the spring, in time for the fall and spring quilt-show seasons. Wouldn't want to have old shoes—there's lots of walking and standing at these shows, and I don't like having tired feet. There are also a few other things I don't like about shows, and I'm going to complain about them right now.

First, the shows are often crowded. Crowds are good for the vendors, *if* the people are the *right* kind of people. Men following their wives around, with their eyes rolling up into their heads in boredom, are *not* the right people, and they are *not* having fun. These poor men should be left at home. Oh, I see, they are there because they like to drive their wives to the show. They feel they are performing a husbandly duty. I understand. My very own husband thinks that driving me to the grocery store and annoying me by taking a half hour to pick out a bottle of salad dressing is performing his husbandly duty. Listen, quit letting them think that. Don't bring non-quilting spouses into the quilt show. Park them in a sports bar or leave them at home. You don't want them seeing everything you buy, and they clog up the aisles, keeping *me* out of the booths.

People with strollers: Don't come on Saturday in the middle of the day. Wait until later in the day or come on a weekday. Your kid is *not* having fun in that stroller. He can't see the stuff for sale; all he can see are the butts around him. That cannot be pleasant. Your stroller is in my way, and I cannot get into the booth.

You! The eight women from the Super Stitchers of Iowa! Go back to your rooms and change clothes. I know you are the Super Stitchers of Iowa because you are all wearing decorated jackets saying so. At one time I found this a cute fashion statement, but I'm over it. In fact, there was a time when I roamed around with a group of women called the Tuesday Night Quilters. We met on Tuesdays, of course. At night. Pat put a flamingo in her front yard one year. It embarrassed her son. He complained; she bought fifty more flamingoes. We had jackets made up with a flamingo holding a sewing needle. Danielle would not wear the jacket; she is French and therefore has good taste in clothing. The rest of us wore them with pride. (I did throw mine out after not having worn it for about a decade. However, Pat's husband—a famous artist—painted her in her jacket, and now I wish I had mine because I could sell it on eBay.) So, the rest of you, pay attention: Grown women do not look good all dressed alike. You are too old for the Brownies. And I know you aren't first graders on a field trip. And, while I'm at it, stop standing in the middle of the aisle showing each other what you just bought. Wait until you get back to your hotel room and have polished off that bottle of wine. You're causing a logjam, and I have nothing else to do but stand there and laugh at your outfits.

You vendors who sell things unrelated to quilting, like floor mops? Knock it off. I don't go to a quilt show to be reminded that I'm not doing any housework. If I wanted to buy a mop, I'd go to a housewares show.

I Love Those Tote Bags

I'm completely comfortable with the green concept of never using plastic bags. And I'm well prepared, because I already have a very large collection of assorted tote bags.

Boy, do I love tote bags. I collect them the way some women collect shoes. I'm probably worse, because I feel no guilt whatsoever.

I've had this obsession for a long time. Shortly after graduating from college, I decided it was time to start wearing makeup to work. My introduction to "gift with purchase" came in the cosmetics department of Marshall Field's (now Macy's). (That's how I refer to it: "Marshall Field's, now Macy's.") I bought some lipstick and eye shadow, got a tote bag filled with some more stuff. Bought facial powder, got a garment bag. I can't remember what the third bag was, but I do recall I came home with three. Brian asked what I bought, and I said, "Makeup. But look, they gave me all this luggage."

I got more use out of the gifts than the makeup. It's been a year since I last succumbed to the gift with purchase, because I finally admitted I still don't like to wear makeup.

When Josh and Sam were toddlers, I found plastic beach totes at the dollar store. Four perfectly filled a grocery cart, and all I had to do at checkout was put the whole bag on the

163

checkout belt and the clerk would repack the groceries right into them. Eventually they all fell apart, but now you can get reusable grocery bags for cheap.

I know this, because I buy them whenever I see them.

When I got a quilt juried into Quilt National in 1999, I think getting a tote bag that said "Quilt National Dairy Barn 1999" was the best part of it. (Besides still getting to brag that I got in.)

I would not be surprised if the promise of tote bags to come was what pulled me into quilting.

I especially like the tote bags they give you at so many quilt shows. Some quilt-show tote bags are quite plain: a simple canvas bag, screen printed with the show's logo and the year. I use these when I'm running errands—outbound mail goes in one, books back to the library in another. Sometimes, they give you a bag with a zipper and pockets. These are a treat.

Last fall, at the big quilt show in Houston, I got the show bag, and then a batting company gave every teacher a canvas bag. The sewing-machine dealer who had supplied the machines for my class gave everyone a small bag, and then he gifted me with another lined bag with zippers, pockets, and a strap. The first thing I did when I got onto the show floor was to buy one more: a model big enough to hold clothes for a weekend. I love this particular manufacturer and this particular size, and I never fly without one, as they fit perfectly in the upper compartment of even the smallest plane and are light enough to go in my suitcase for shopping on trips. I can't remember what else I bought that trip. Oh yes, there's the purse I got when my friend Francis and I went to the Asian store behind the convention center. She bought small purses, one in every color they had, to hold her beads, and she treated me to one in blue.

My husband goes to an industry show every year and surrenders his tote bag to me. It says "Disaster Recovery Journal Fall Show." Sometimes I cover up the last three words so it just says "Disaster Recovery," which reminds me how much better quilting makes me feel.

We went to a boat show last week. I was disappointed that the show bag was not free, or that interesting. We didn't buy a new boat, but of course, I got a bag. A ditty bag, with forty-nine pockets on the inside. The choice of colors was plain canvas, black fabric, or hot pink fabric with lime green straps. I'm sure you know that I bought the pink and green. But not after telling the vendor that black with green straps would be a big seller at quilt shows.

I hope we get started sailing again soon. It's been twenty years, but if I remember correctly, we used a lot of canvas bags to hold stuff. I wonder if anyone will think it odd that all the storage bags have quilt logos on them.

The Waffle Incident

Because most of my teaching involves traveling to a quilt show or group, I spend quite a bit of time in hotels. My favorite hotels give you free breakfast, and they often have those nifty waffle makers. I love them, but it's taken me several tries to figure them out. The first time, I poured the batter out of the premeasured cup into the maker and just stood there, and nothing happened. I finally figured out you have to flip them over to get them started and then wait for the very loud buzzer to go off before your pry them out with a weird-shaped plastic fork. In Payson, Arizona, you poured the batter out of a pitcher into a cup, and I poured too much, so the extra just ran off, but my waffle was perfect. In Fountain Hills, Arizona, they didn't have premeasured cups, or a pitcher, they had a dispenser, much like the juice dispensers you see everywhere.

I looked at it carefully. The spout had a sticker that said it was *not* disposable. I wasn't planning to throw it out. There was a picture above the spout that showed the little lever on the top of the spout and said "push." So, I held a cup under the spout and pushed, gently. The spout fell off. The batter filled up my cup and started running all over the counter. I jammed the spout back in place, stopping the flow of batter, and said, "A Lucy and Ethel moment." Often, there is someone in the breakfast area in charge of everything. I looked around; no one in sight who appeared to be paying attention. Another guest came over and tried to help stem the river of batter that was approaching the edge of the counter. She gave up and went to get the attendant. I noticed that the spout was turned sideways and the other end needed to be screwed back into the dispenser, so I *turned* it, and more batter blooped out. I got the spout on quickly and tried to screw it on, with no success, so I just stood there until the attendant came. She put a pitcher under the spout, took it off, and the pitcher overflowed. At this point, she gave up and let the batter run onto the floor. The maintenance man finally got the spout back on, unfortunately after the batter had emptied into a large puddle. He said, "What did you do?" more puzzled than angry. I said all I did was "push" and that I suspected the spout hadn't been screwed on tightly. He laughed, cleaned up the batter, and I had cereal for breakfast.

The next morning, I looked at the dispenser; the maintenance man came over and said, "It's safe." I had cereal anyway.

Just like getting back on the horse that throws you, I have since made waffles in hotels. I shy away from the dispensers, but if they have premeasured cups, I'm good. Very good. I'd say I'm a perfect waffle maker. Not that I do anything besides pour and turn, but I am very good at waiting for that timer to go off by looking over the buffet for other things to go with my waffle, such as fruity syrupy stuff like strawberries and blueberries. And whipped cream. Nothing like having dessert for breakfast to get the day off to a good start.

Buoyed by my hotel success, I wanted to do this at home. Sam and Josh bought me a waffle maker for Christmas. I carefully mixed the batter, exactly as directed, and, exactly as told, poured one and three quarter cups onto the grid. Not a smidge more or less. Exactly one and three quarter cups of batter. Alas, three quarters of a cup flowed off the grid, onto my counter. Lovely waffle though. I tried again with less batter. Still made a mess. I put a tray under the waffle iron, to catch the runoff. A lot of good that did—the batter just ran directly onto the floor. Finally, on my last waffle, I got it right: exactly three quarters of a cup, poured into the center.

My son's girlfriend arrived at the front door just as I got the last waffle on a plate. I'd never met her before. I offered her the waffle, and she accepted. No matter what happens next, as least she thinks I can make a great waffle.

Going to See Mount Rushmore

I admire the national teachers who know how to dress well for quilt shows. Some of them excel at wearables, so day after day, they display their creative skills on their own bodies. Others dress very professionally, as if they are going to a business meeting. I don't have my act together, wardrobe wise.

I keep trying. It makes it easier to pack for a trip if you have a regular image to present. My first problem is that I have foot issues: I can't wear high heels, or even dressy flat shoes. I have to wear shoes that accommodate my orthotics and give my feet extra cushioning. For me, a certain brand of athletic shoes are the only ones that work. Luckily, it is often said that "fashion stops at the knees" at quilt shows because of so much walking. I have given myself permission to wear whatever shoes will keep me from being in pain by the end of the day.

One year, I regularly wore a pair of lime green gym shoes, like the ones I had in grade school. People noticed them, as lime green footwear wasn't that common back then. I was going to be teaching in Washington, DC, at a fabric store that catered to an upscale clientele—including the political set, who would go there with their tailor to buy $200-a-yard

Chantilly lace for dinners at the White House. (At least that was what I imagined the fabric was for.) I thought it would be nice to dress somewhat formally but couldn't bring myself to do it. Instead, I bought a feathered boa at a crafts store and wore that with a velvet dress and my lime green gym shoes. I made quite an impression, especially walking down the street to the shop. Perhaps passers by thought I was an eccentric homeless person. Or a relative of Phyllis Diller. Actually, Phyllis was my inspiration for the outfit.

Since I dye my own fabric, I should be able to whip up a wardrobe of comfortable, colorful, cotton clothes, but I'm not that great at sewing clothes. I've tried buying white clothes and dyeing them, which worked well for a few years. Everywhere I went, I wore tie-dyed golf shirts.

I have somewhat of a standardized wardrobe, at least for a while, in the summer: interesting T-shirts that I have collected during my quilting travels. Quite often there is an official T-shirt for a specific quilt show, and when I see those, I immediately grab them. Sometimes a guild presents me with a shirt from a show they held earlier in the year. My current favorite is from the guild in Tucson, Arizona. It's black, with images of chili peppers, and says "Quilt Fiesta!" They gave it to me on the first day of my booking with them, and I wore it the second day to teach. At the end of the day, I stopped in the hotel's bar for the free hors d'oeuvres, and the bartender was quite taken with the shirt. He probably didn't notice it said "Quilt" on it and wanted to know where he could get one. I told him he'd have to go to a quilt show.

The Gulf States Quilting Association featured shirts in lime green, and since that is my favorite color, I even wear it when I'm in Chicago. People assume I'm a tourist.

A few years ago, I was teaching in Rapid City, South Dakota. My hostess lived about an hour out of town, on the edge of a national park. She felt strongly that one cannot visit Rapid City without visiting "The Boys" at Mount Rushmore. The plan was to eat dinner there after finishing up the class for the day. When we drove into town in the morning, to start the class, her car died right as we pulled into the parking lot. Luckily her mother was game to see "The Boys" too, and offered to drive us. Her mother felt that one cannot visit Rapid City without stopping in nearby Sturgis to get a T-shirt commemorating "Bike Week," the annual motorcycle rally in the Black Hills. I agreed this was a necessity and off we went. I picked out several shirts: one for the current year's rally, another for the past year (it was on sale), one for my son, and one for my daughter, all at the hotel next to the truck stop. My shirts are very cool— flaming skulls and flaming skeletons riding Harleys. We were done with that about seven o'clock at night, and off we went to Mount Rushmore.

My hostess's mother also felt strongly that since our path would take us through Deadwood, a town featured in the same-named series on HBO, we had to stop there too, to see the town and gamble in a few of the casinos, especially in the hotel that was always on the show. Not having a clue about the time frame involved, and not wanting to be rude or anything, I agreed. I didn't buy any T-shirts in Deadwood, but I did win five dollars at an Elvis Presley slot machine. I bought a few souvenirs there for Josh, as he was taking a class on Elvis Presley that year in college. (Ironic that I had to work so hard to pay his tuition while he took goofy classes like that, but we won't go there.)

We got back to the car at about ten o'clock and headed off to Mount Rushmore. I finally looked at a map and realized we had driven a very long distance—first north to Sturgis, then south to Deadwood—and still had a long way to go. GPS would have been a good thing to have at that point but, alas, we didn't and got lost a few times. We finally rolled up to the gates at Mount Rushmore at eleven o'clock. They were locked. No lights were on "The Boys." Oh well. I'd have to see them the next trip. My hostess's mother began the drive home. I consulted the map; we were driving through a national forest. The road was narrow; literally every one hundred feet, there was a tunnel cut out of the rock, only one lane going through it, and then there would be an extremely sharp turn to avoid going over the cliff. A lot of horn honking was required, even though it was midnight. I would have been terrified to be the driver. As it was, I was tired but afraid to go to sleep in case I woke up as the car was flying off a precipice. We got home at about one in the morning, just in time to have a quick meal and a short nap before my hostess's mother drove me to the airport for my six o'clock flight to Minneapolis, where I was teaching later in the week. I was impressed that my hostess's mother was able to drive so far on so little sleep. She told me that she'd been doing it all her life. She was quite a woman.

I love wearing the biker shirts, because I am so not a biker chick, and I get funny reactions. One of the postal clerks in my hometown post office is a rider. He noticed my shirt as I was walking away from his counter and called out, "Hey great shirt! Did you go?"

"Of course not," I replied. "Just went to Rapid City to get the shirt."

I collected some shirts from a restaurant called Round the Bend Steakhouse in South Bend, Nebraska, on the way between a lecture in Lincoln and a class in Omaha. I thought my kids would enjoy them, as the restaurant is the home of the annual Testicle Festival. I think you can imagine what is on the menu.

I haven't managed to find just the right quilting event to display that shirt. Maybe the next time I go to see Mount Rushmore.

Don't Call Me

I'm writing this while sitting at the local Panera Bread restaurant. They have free wireless internet access, as well as infinite refills on soft drinks. I met my friend Kathleen here for lunch, ate with her, chatted for a few hours, and then she left. Now here I am on my own, ready to write, if I could just concentrate.

I'm sitting at a table in the back of the restaurant, in a room that I thought was the quiet room. There's a nice guy here—he's friendly and will watch my laptop while I run to the bathroom, which I have to do every five minutes, due to the infinite Diet Pepsi refills. Here's the problem: He's on his cell phone. I've got my sound-canceling ear buds in; I'm listening to a nice selection of piano solos. The plan is to sit here until I write something. At home, I keep finding other things to do (stuff I normally wouldn't be bothered with, like the laundry). I wrote my first book at the Baker's Square, another restaurant, but I thought this would be better since they have free Internet.

Anyway, I'm having a problem because this guy keeps talking and talking and talking on his cell phone, loud enough to break through the music and the sound canceling. That's pretty loud, because these headphones keep small, whiny children on airplanes from annoying me.

Secondhand cell phone conversations really irritate me. Actually, firsthand cell phone conversations—the ones in which I have to talk to someone—don't thrill me either. I have a cell phone (I'm not a total Luddite), but not a really cool one like the iPhone. I have a phone my son bought as a present for me at Target. I pay by the minute. I used sixty dollars worth of cell phone time last year. When I had a phone with three hundred minutes, it cost sixty dollars per month, and people would call me. And expect me to call them. If I wanted to talk on the phone, I'd stay home. When I'm out, I want to be left alone. I especially don't want calls from my husband or kids asking when I'll be home. Usually these calls come as I am pulling into the driveway. The kids have a firm grip on the concept of not calling me; it came about when I would answer by saying, "Did you have a car accident? Or another emergency? Because I pay for this by the minute, you know." They do call me at home, on the "real" phone. It seems like Sam cannot stand to wait for a bus without something to do, so she calls me. And then abruptly ends the conversation when the transportation arrives. That used to get on my nerves too, but now I'm happy that she cares enough to call once in a while and just chat without asking for money or to announce an emergency.

Still, I really don't have that much attachment to cell phones. I think people should be able to be out of touch once in a while. I have to fly a lot to get to quilt shows and teaching gigs with quilt guilds. If they start allowing cell phone calls during flights, I'll have to find another occupation.

The irritation of the secondhand cell phone begins at the gate. There are some businessmen who seem to think that everyone will be very impressed if they spend their time waiting for the plane making important phone calls. Usually, the annoyance stops when the flight attendant tells everyone to turn off their phones because the cabin door is shut, but that is not always the case.

Last summer, I was flying to Duluth, Minnesota, for a quilt show. The trip was going to take two flights; the first from Chicago to Minneapolis, leaving at 6:30 a.m. on a Wednesday. Normally, O'Hare isn't that crowded at the crack of dawn, but that day was different. It was right after the suspected terrorists were arrested in London, the week that the ban on liquids was instituted. Going through security, normally a quick trip, took forty minutes; then I had to chug my coffee at McDonald's, because you could buy coffee in the airport but not bring it on the plane. By the time I got to the plane headed for Duluth, I was cranky, tired, and hungry, but trying to make the best of it.

The plane was a small jet—the kind you have to walk up stairs to get onto. The kind of plane that is really more like a skateboard with wings. When I got to my seat, I looked up, and a bee was hovering around the luggage compartment. The guy across the aisle noticed it too.

"What do you think happens to a bee when it's on a plane? Do you think it can still fly?" I asked him. He looked at me oddly. "I mean, you know how they communicate with their fellow bees about where the honey is, by doing an elaborate dance when they get back to the hive? What if they get off the plane in Duluth instead of Minneapolis and can't find their hive? What happens then?" The guy just continued to look at me. "The movie *Snakes on a Plane* opens this week. I wonder if bees panic on a plane." He just stared. I gave up; obviously, he was not interested in conversation this early.

The flight attendant, who looked to be about thirteen years old (although I'm sure she was much older—at least twenty-one) announced that the cabin door was now closed and all electronics and cell phones were to be shut off. Seat backs should be upright and tray tables put away. She then went through her safety presentation. I was probably the only one watching. I always watch the flight attendants do their safety thing; I read somewhere that if you pay attention, no matter how often you fly, you'll have a better chance of making it off a burning plane alive. It's like it gets something in gear in your brain, ready to go at a moment's notice. So I watched the preteen flight attendant do her thing, and then she sat down at the front of the plane and belted herself into a jump seat as the plane pulled away from the gate.

At that moment, the guy in the seat in front of me leaned his seat back almost into my lap. I tried to remember if this endangered him or me. Would this cause him to go flying backwards in case of a bad takeoff, or was I the one threatened by the inability to bend forward and put my head between my knees? (Not that I can do that anyway.)

While I pondered what to do about the leaning seat offender, the guy directly behind me answered his cell phone.

"Yes, I'm on the plane. We're about to take off. Weather is good. So how is your family?"

Did this guy not remember that phones were *verboten*? Did he not realize we were *moving*? I didn't get up at three in the morning and go through an hour-long security check just so this guy could talk on his cell phone, endangering the lives of everyone else on the plane.

I turned around. "Sir, you aren't supposed to be using a phone. Please turn it off." He just looked at me, sorta like the guy across the aisle had. And continued talking. "Yes, the meeting is at two. Um hum. Yes. . . ."

I turned around and slapped his knee, because that was all I could reach. "HEY! TURN YOUR PHONE OFF *NOW*!"

He said into his phone, "I gotta go."

Now the guy in the aisle next to him was looking at me and smiling. Not the guy who thought I was odd about the bees. This guy was behind him. I couldn't decide if the smiling guy thought I was a nut job or if he appreciated me telling the phone guy to knock it off.

I spent the rest of the flight thinking up the best thing to say to Mr. Cellphone. "If you are so important that you can't be incommunicado for an hour, perhaps you should arrange for use of your corporate jet." (I use very flowery language when I'm ticked off and defensive.) "You must have a very high self image if you think your phone conversation is more important than the lives of the other thirty people on this plane."

He never said anything to me, and instead of talking to him, I blocked his way off the plane while my seatmate woke up slowly and grabbed her stuff.

This episode caused me some stress for the next few days. I wondered what was wrong that I was picking on strangers in public. I mentioned it to my husband, and he said the smiling guy was probably happy that I told the phone guy off. He would have been, he said.

In any case, on the way home, I resolved to control my temper better, and I have to say the nun who sat across the aisle from me didn't try anything stupid.

I told this story to a flight attendant sitting next to me on a flight later in the year. She said that cell phones do, indeed, interfere with the radio on small planes; the pilot can't always hear the control tower. Vindication. Later in the year, on another flight, on a very *large* plane, I overheard the head flight attendant tell another crewmember to go back to seat 23A and confiscate their phone. We were ascending. She said the pilot was *very angry* and he wanted that phone off *now*.

I felt vindicated. Now if only they had flight attendants at this restaurant to discipline the cell phone users so I could write in peace.

Teacher Reviews

Brian and I were eating dinner in a steakhouse last week. The waiter was being very attentive, giving us good advice on which steaks to order (the area is well known for its beef) and answering our questions about some of the local politics. He even brought me a piece of chocolate cake with a birthday candle on it. We were in Canada, and it was the first night of the Stanley Cup playoffs. I was wearing a T-shirt bearing the logo of the local hockey team on the front and the goalie—their star player—on the back. I assumed his excellent service was due to the fact that it was my birthday, he thought I was a hockey fan, and he was a nice guy. I'm sure all those are true; however, when the bill came, there was an evaluation form along with the credit-card slip. We rated the server excellent on every point; I even wrote comments praising him in the spaces provided, using a lot of exclamation points. I'm sure it had nothing to do with the fact that I'd been drinking local beer on tap along with my steak.

It's a good thing I don't have to be a waiter, because I couldn't do it. Aside from the fact that I'm sure I'd drop every other meal on some innocent diner, I couldn't take the exposure to constant critique.

Many of the quilt shows, and some of the guilds, where I have taught pass out critique sheets to the students. These make me crazy. Some of the other teachers look at them as a way to learn how to improve their teaching, and I'll agree that once in a while there is a suggestion I can run with. More often than not, that isn't the case.

One early critique I received said, "Great quilter. Terrible teacher." Nothing else. Thanks a lot. What can I do with that information besides cancel all my engagements and hide in my studio? I haven't gotten a critique that horrible in a long time, but I still do get hurtful comments. I've found that if I read them every day after class, I react in an odd way and get very defensive the next morning when I start teaching again.

Other teachers have given me excellent advice on how to deal with the critiques. Some save all of the critiques and read them all at once. I've done that, but even if 140 people out of 150 are completely happy, those 10 people who had some complaint upset me.

I think that people writing the critiques aren't really thinking about how their comments will be received; they write things they wouldn't say to a teacher face to face.

Perhaps they think they are being helpful. Because they are handed the critique form on the way into class, this puts them in a critical frame of mind right from the start. It can be hard to overcome as the teacher.

My favorite critique came from a class given at a brand new venue. We were squashed into a classroom that was too small, the tables were narrow, and there was no room to move, let alone work comfortably. I started out by telling the students that any comments on the critique sheet would be read by the people running the show and suggested we make the best out of a bad situation and try to enjoy ourselves. While some people did use the space to complain about the classroom, one woman wrote, "On the Luncheon/Supper: Chicken, chicken, chicken, WHY ALL THE CHICKEN?"

Students certainly have a right to voice their concerns. They've spent a lot of money to pay for the class and pay to travel there, and they've spent precious hours that could have been used for shopping or looking at quilts.

Students come into a classroom with different expectations. Some want to be presented with an avalanche of material, in a structured format, with everyone doing the same thing at the same time. I do not teach like that. I present a demonstration and then let students work, while I walk around and give each student individual attention.

Some students take their classes as seriously as if they were going to work. Others consider a day in a quilt class to be a day of entertainment. I'm with the latter group.

I've come to the conclusion that I am who I am, and the people who take my classes can get a good idea of what they are in for by reading my columns, my books, or my website. I owe it to students to have the best designs I can offer them; to demonstrate the best techniques; to show up ready to teach, having taken a shower; and to be pleasant.

Some days I wish I could fill out a critique for each student. Did they bother to read the supply list and come to class with the right materials? Did they come in with a bad mood and take it out on everyone around them? If they know so much, why are they taking the class instead of teaching it?

At least I don't have to work for tips.

Fear of Speaking

Public speaking is big on the list of things people fear the most. For me, that is not true. I like public speaking. Perhaps I just need the attention.

A long time ago, I wanted to be president of my quilt guild—not because I have a need to control things, but because I wanted to be up on the podium running the guild meeting so that I could crack jokes. After two years of being president (and paying attention to the speakers we hired), it dawned on me that I could be a traveling lecturer and make money to crack wise, instead of having to spend the better portion of a year doing administrative tasks in order to have five minutes of time in front of one guild.

Also, if I traveled, the other guilds wouldn't have already heard the same jokes.

There are some scary parts about giving a quilt lecture. I normally fly to a speaking engagement, so I can't bring all of my quilts with me. I used to do slide lectures, using an old-fashioned slide projector, while many of my colleagues moved on to using digital projectors. Even though I love to use computers, I have noticed that whenever someone else is watching me use my computer, something goes wrong. I was also worried that the image produced by the digital projector wouldn't be as good as the slide projector. (After I bought a digital projector, it took me two years before I could overcome these fears and start using it.) But three lectures in a row helped me renounce slide projectors for good.

The first lecture was held in a church. There was no projector screen; they wanted me to show the lecture on a wall. I had to aim the projector so that I wasn't covering up the crucifix with images of my quilts. Plus, it was a concrete block wall, which is not flat. The second lecture was given to a guild that had borrowed a slide projector from a library. It had no remote, it had lots of dust buildup, and it started eating my slides. When I nearly electrocuted myself trying to pull a slide out of the tray while it was still plugged in, because I was nervous and using a tweezers, I thought about making the switch to digital. After the third lecture, when all three things occurred—no screen, no remote, projector eating my slides—I made the switch.

In my opinion, the problem with digital projectors is that the replacement bulbs are *very* expensive—usually around four hundred dollars. I am loath to buy one and carry it around, so I have a constant fear that my bulb will burn out in the middle of a lecture and I'll have to wave my hands around for the rest of the hour. However, I have recently purchased an older digital projector from a fellow teacher, who *did* buy the extra bulb, and now I have two projectors and three bulbs. So I should be good.

The next fear I have is falling off the stage and hurting myself. I am not the most graceful person, and it is not an unlikely event. Once, at my own guild, I suddenly discovered that the podium rolled very easily. I was leaning on it at the time, standing on a stool. That's another problem with podiums for me; I am so short that if I stand behind one, the audience cannot see me. I try to stand next to them now.

In Australia, I was the keynote speaker for a quilt symposium. Before my speech, food and drink was served, including champagne. I had a few glasses. Having something to drink is not always a bad idea before a lecture. I know that my audience certainly laughs easier when *they've* had a few (which is one reason I love being the banquet speaker). Anyway, I had some champagne, but I promise I wasn't drunk. The stage was painted black. The auditorium was very dark. The lights shining on me were very bright, and I could not see much. I had a quilt showing on the screen at the back of the stage and walked over to point at a detail. Unfortunately, the stage ended about a foot before the screen began. I discovered this when I started falling off the back of the stage. My fall was stopped by a shelf, also painted black, that magically appeared out of nowhere. All I knew was that I was no longer falling, I had made a huge thud, and my arm hurt. But not that much. My biggest fear was that everyone would think I was drunk. The lecture went on without further incident, and everybody laughed and enjoyed themselves. So, now, I just make sure I know where the stage ends, what moves, and what doesn't.

My main concern when lecturing is to keep everyone laughing. Theoretically, if I am giving a quilt lecture, the purpose is to show my quilts and educate the audience about how I make them. In my mind though, the quilts are simply there as the excuse I have for standing up in front of a bunch of people and trying to get them to laugh. I have always enjoyed cracking people up, sometimes when I am not supposed to. I used to get in trouble for talking in class when I was a child, and I still annoy people in circumstances where I am supposed to be quiet and fade into the background. I would have loved to be a standup comic and, for me, giving a quilt lecture is probably as close as I am going to get. I have thought about trying standup, but I'm afraid to. The thing about a quilt lecture is that the audience is not expecting to laugh, so for them, that's a bonus. (Unless they have already heard that my reputation is to be entertaining, and then they are already on my side anyway.) Standing in a bar full of paying customers waiting to be entertained, however, is not a good plan for me.

I have noticed that the bigger the audience, the easier it is to get them to laugh. Especially, as I mentioned before, if it is a banquet, and they've had some wine, or perhaps a long day shopping for quilt supplies at a show, whatever—they are usually happy. If there are three hundred people in the audience and only 10 percent laugh, that is still thirty people laughing. In a small group of, say, thirty people, 10 percent laughing is only three people. I can hear thirty people laughing better than three, and that makes me feel more self-confident.

They say that the best way to start a lecture or speech is with a joke. I use a quilt that I made about fifteen years ago as a prop and introduce myself. I try to get someone else to hold it up, usually someone I have pegged ahead of time as a good sport. Last year, I asked the husband of one of the show organizers to hold up my quilt. While I was talking, I noticed that they were projecting my live image, much larger than life, on a screen to one side of the stage. I looked very fat. I moved the guy, the quilt, and myself to the other side of the stage so I wouldn't have to look at myself. I stood behind the podium and said, "Do I look thinner now?" To me, the lecture had already started, and it was going well. The man seemed a bit perplexed; I think he thought I was going to be very professional and immediately launch into an educational speech. Instead, I was talking about how badly I get PMS each month, as that is the topic of the quilt. Suddenly, his cell phone rang. He answered it, and as I stood there, I kept thinking, "There has to be a really funny line in this. If only I could come up with it." I started laughing, not coming up with the line. Everyone else started laughing too. If it had been anyone but the "Boss's husband," I might have asked to speak to the caller myself. He finally hung up, and I went on with my lecture. Afterward, several people told me they assumed I had planned that.

Some of the best starts to my lectures happen when something goes wrong and I have to talk and fix things at the same time. One time I decided that the lecture room would not be dark enough to use my projector, as it was part of an exhibition hall, separated from the rest of the quilt show only by drapes. I pulled out the package of old-fashioned slides I carry with me for just such an emergency and put them in the tray. They started falling out faster than I could get them in. I eventually got everything working when a voice came from the PA system, announcing that the show was closed. I asked the audience if they heard the voice too. Indeed, of course, they did. Then, the lights finally dimmed. The whole thing was chaotic, and I was disconcerted, but I kept going.

After that episode, I thought about setting up a lecture where everything goes wrong on purpose, but I don't think that would work for me. Everything that was supposed to go wrong wouldn't, and new problems would introduce themselves. I'll just keep going as I am: slightly on the edge of disaster at all times. I had one student who was at the show I just mentioned come back the next year to take a class from me. She said that if I was that funny during a lecture, the class had to be good. Luckily, I don't remember anything too chaotic happening during the class.

CHAPTER FIVE

Quilting:

The Universal Language

Talking to Strangers

One thing I love about big quilt shows is that everybody wears a nametag. Your nametag will have your name (obviously), your town, and often what your "job" is at the quilt show. If you are a vendor, it will say your company, or if you are teaching, it announces that too. If the show administration doesn't give you a nametag, you are welcome to bring your own. If you belong to a quilting guild, you probably have one already.

What I like about the nametags is that they give me a great excuse to talk to strangers. Okay, I have to admit that I talk to strangers all the time anyway, but at least in a quilt-show setting, it's more acceptable and people won't back off thinking you're a weirdo. Well, there was that woman in line at the coat check one year, in Chicago, my own hometown, who was taken aback when I asked her if I could sign her tote bag. She had just explained to another friend that she was asking teachers to sign it. My name was not on there, so I offered to autograph it. "Who are you?" she asked. I explained that I was teaching. She said it would be okay if I signed, but she didn't seem that thrilled. I amuse myself by daydreaming that when she told a friend about the woman who insisted on defacing her tote bag, her friend explained to her it was

Robbi Eklow, Goddess of the Last Minute, and she should be completely delighted and forever cherish the tote bag as an heirloom.

Usually, though, a nametag with "Instructor" printed on it indicates that I am part of the "Establishment" of the show, and by talking to people, I am merely doing my job in making them feel welcome. In other words, I pretend that not only am I being paid to teach a class, I am being paid to engage strangers, who are busy shopping in booths, in conversation. And it's also a valid excuse to eat lunch with whoever else has a nametag on. Quilters are very friendly, and when we are at quilt shows having fun, I would say 99 percent of the quilting population is open to random conversation from other quilters.

Often there are buses running back and forth between hotels and the convention centers where the quilt shows are being held. We get on the bus and immediately talk to the person sitting next to us. We look at their nametag and perhaps make a comment about a friend we know who lives near their hometown, or ask them if they are enjoying the show. We tell each other how long we have been quilting, how many times we've come to this show, who we came with, where we are staying, and what we plan to do later. By the time the five-minute bus ride is over, we've made a new friend. Just try getting on public transportation and asking your seatmate where she is from (because she isn't wearing a nametag that introduces her), how her day went, what kind of hobbies she has, where she lives, etc. They'll probably arrest you.

Quilters are friendly like this back at home too. Other fiber and craft people are also like that. One evening, I was waiting for two friends to show up at a restaurant for dinner before our guild meeting. A woman walked by, about fifty feet away. She was wearing a fabulous beaded necklace. I thought she was a fellow quilter, coming to the restaurant for dinner. I got up off the bench and ran over to her, told her how much I loved her necklace, and asked if I could look at it closer. She let me, a complete stranger, stand there feeling the fringe on her necklace. I asked her if she was looking forward to the guild meeting. What guild meeting? Uh oh, she was *not* a fellow guild member. But she *was* a beader and therefore didn't think I was trying to mug her. Unlike that woman in the airport who had a fabulous purse made out of a cigar box. *She* moved backwards in horror as I came toward her to examine the purse. That was back when most items that had the look of being handmade actually were. Now you can never be sure that someone sporting unusual wearable art made it him or herself, or even bought it from an artist—it could come from any chain store.

To be safe, you might want to remember to only paw at the clothing or jewelry of other quilters wearing nametags.

I prefer the nametags that hang around your neck instead of being pinned to a jacket. I usually wear a beaded necklace at the same time, and quite often I forget at the end of the day that I still have my nametag on. My friends tease me when we are no longer at the quilt show, or in the bus on the way to the hotel, and I'm wandering around still wearing my nametag. Once I was in a hardware store wearing a nametag that said "Hi! I'm Robbi!" and some guy, not an employee, came up to me and said, "Hi Robbi! What are you shopping for?" (However, had he done that in a quilt shop, we could have had a nice discussion about batik fabrics.)

Sometimes people who say hello to me aren't quilters but know who I am. That's a bit startling to me. At a very large quilt show, an older man came up to me and said "Robbi! I knew that was you! I recognized your voice!" Was this my long-lost father? No, it was some guy whose wife watches *Simply Quilts* on TV every morning during breakfast. Apparently my one segment on the show had played often enough that he knew my voice.

Last year, I was staying in a hotel about two blocks from a quilt show. One morning I was in the elevator after going to the gym. Not showered yet, no nametag. My lime green T-shirt was dirty. I apologized for being a slob to the two women who got in the elevator. "Well, at least it's your favorite color!" said one of them. How did she know that? I never figured it out, but I think I better make sure I take a shower before wandering around the hotel in the morning.

Many of the quilt shows have a ribbon that sticks on the nametag; for example, "Instructor" or "Faculty" for the teachers, "Vendor" for the vendors, "Exhibitor" if you have a quilt in the show. If your quilt won a ribbon, very often you get a matching ribbon to wear while you are at the show. Those are the best, because we know you are happy about your ribbon and will welcome any compliments we care to give you as a conversation opener. Some shows give first-time visitors a special ribbon to wear. I presume so that the veterans among us can welcome them. Wouldn't it be fun if everyone had a ribbon everywhere you went? At the hardware store, "I'm here to fix the sink myself!" Grocery store, "I'm cooking a three-course dinner for my family!" Bowling alley, "I just learned to bowl! And these are rented shoes!"

Maybe if we all wore nametags with our names or accomplishments, instead of wearing the name of a clothing designer or store, the world would be a friendlier place. Wouldn't you rather congratulate the guy in the checkout line for making dessert tonight instead of silently acknowledging that he bought his shirt from a famous designer?

Conversation at the Post Office

The conversation at the post office started like this:

Postal clerk: Would you like insurance for this package?

Robbi: How much would that cost?

Postal clerk: About two dollars.

Robbi: That's okay, I've sent small quilts by priority mail without insurance, and they are worth a lot more.

Postal Clerk: You make quilts? I'm a quilter too.

At that point, all conversation about the insurance was intertwined with talking about quilts. The postal clerk told me which quilt shop she goes to, and that she is making a baby quilt for her niece, but she doesn't know what pattern to use, as the girl is about nine years old.

There was a line of patrons waiting, but we were away from the main counter, at one of those side corners they have in some of the post offices—the kind where they sell tote bags, framed stamps, and other types of gifts. The people at the front of the line were probably out of earshot. If not, at least we couldn't see if they were visibly annoyed by the slowdown caused by our quilting conversation.

I suggested she try making half-square triangles and drew the instructions on a sheet of paper she handed me. Then she remembered to charge me for the postage and the insurance. I figured that now that it had been brought up, I had to buy insurance or else the package would get lost. Not that the postal clerk was threatening me, but because whenever I decide to worry about something and then decide it won't happen, it happens. Plus it had been one of those weeks; this was my second trip to ship off this box. The first time I'd forgotten to bring the invoice with the mailing address (it was sitting neatly at home on my computer desk). I didn't want to think the box was cursed, so I bought the insurance.

As she rung me up, she said, "I should be paying *you* for the lesson. Do you teach?" I told her that I teach for guilds and at shows, and suggested she read my column in *Quilting Arts*. She wrote that down and then said, "Do you come here often?" I do, I told her, but this wasn't my "home" post office; I use it when I'm going to the library. "Well, I hope you'll come by again soon so we can talk about quilts some more."

When I first started submitting quilts to juried shows, I was certain that one specific clerk at my regular post office, Kathy, was my good look charm, and I would let people go ahead of me in order to get her "magic" stamp on my envelope. I stopped sealing the entries until after Kathy had a chance to examine the slides. Kathy sent me to the new quilt shop in town as soon as it opened. Kathy was like that; she'd always take the time to chat with her customers. It probably didn't make for the most efficient post office in town—well, actually it was the *only* post office in town—but it was nice to get to know her over the years. Kathy retired, and since not every entry (specifically Quilt National entries) got in just because she approved them, I'm okay with going to the first clerk open.

I'm at the post office quite often, mailing books, patterns, quilt-show entries, quilts. Some things are ready to go but need to be handed to a real person. My current running conversation with the clerks is about what tattoo to get to commemorate my fiftieth birthday and where to get it (both on my body and which parlor to go to). One of the clerks is a biker, and he has a lot of tattoos and good information. Maybe I should designate him my new lucky clerk.

A Fibery Day at the Dentist

I went to the dentist today for two reasons. First, last fall, I thought I broke off part of a back tooth. It didn't hurt, and I went out of town and forgot about it until about a month before my dental checkup. I asked the dentist if I had had a mishap or imagined it. Yes, a tiny bit was missing from a filling, and it took along a piece of tooth. I needed to take care of that today. Also, I needed a new mouth guard to wear at night, or else I grind my teeth. And I snore.

He is making a mouth guard for me that will keep me from breaking all my teeth at night and will help with the snoring. I have tried other methods, like those sticky things you put on the outside of your nose. Other quilt teachers who share rooms with me at quilt shows have informed me that those don't seem to be working that well. Brian is no help; when I ask him if they seem to make a difference, he says that either he doesn't hear me because he goes to sleep first, or that it's cute when I snore and not that noisy. (When I'm not fixating about it, he has said that he could tell I was tired when he left for work, because I was sawing away. So the man cannot make up his mind.)

I have been friends with Lynn, who runs the dental office, since we were in high school. In between talking about our kids, we compare notes on our fiber habits. We both knit, bead, and quilt. Lynn wanted to learn how to do the peyote stitch and was planning to take a class. All of the books she had weren't helping. I told her I could teach her in five minutes if I had some beads. When Lauren called to remind me of the appointment, she also said she had a note from Lynn that I should bring beads.

When I arrived at the dentist, I had a tote bag full of beading supplies. We let the dentist give me the shot of Novocain and while we waited for it to numb me up, Lynn came and sat on the dentist's stool. I suggested she thread the needle, as it takes me a long time at this point. Lynn tried, but the thread was too thick.

"Bite it and make it thinner," I told her.

"You aren't supposed to use your teeth as a tool," she said as she bit the thread gently and threaded the needle.

We needed a work surface to lay out the beads. "We'll use the dental tray, and I'll switch the cover when you are numb," Lynn said. We did that and also used the very excellent light that dentists have hanging right there.

The dentist came in and offered the use of his magnifying glasses. I asked him if he ever made jewelry and, in fact, he did before dental school—quite a bit of it.

I'm not sure how long Lynn's lesson took, but now I can say that I can teach someone to weave beads in the time it takes Novocain to start working.

When the assistant who made up the necessary impressions for the mouth guard came in, she said she needed to know how much I weigh. I grimaced and told her.

She thought I was joking and said, "Really, I need your weight."

I said, "Yes, I'm lying. I really weigh 120 pounds and I'm telling that other number just for fun."

She laughed and then did the impressions very quickly. I was impressed. I asked her what they make them out of. Seaweed. Aha! I told her that I use the same stuff to thicken dye.

When I was leaving, Lynn introduced me to another patient who was doing an afghan using a new tool I hadn't seen before that gives you a double layer of crochet.

I remarked that coming to the dentist was just like coming to a fiber emporium. Who knew? Then I left to see if I could visit the knitting store she mentioned before my Novocain wore off.

A block before the knitting store, I noticed a small sign announcing a new quilt shop. I couldn't turn fast enough and had to double back, then do it again, as I missed it the second time too. I finally got there on the third try. What a cute new store! And I had a wonderful conversation with another quilter I hadn't seen in about five years.

All in all, it was a very fibery day. And here I thought I was just going to the dentist.

A Quilter Walks into a Hardware Store

I belong to a critique group. We meet about once a month, at Beth's house. I don't go for the critique part that much—I find I don't have anything intelligent to say about the others' quilts, beyond telling them how fabulous they are, and how they will surely win a prize. (Then I go to the next meeting and tell them I was right about the prize, wasn't I?) No, the critique isn't the thing. I go because I like the other quilters' company, Beth puts out a very nice snack spread, and I like to sit on the floor and eat crackers and cheese off the coffee table. And because Beth makes excellent cider in the winter.

I try to bring quilts to share, but for the last few months, I haven't finished anything. My current quilt is still under construction. Literally. I took a big piece of fabric, about seven feet by seven feet, and pinned it to my working wall. Then I staked out a sixty-five-inch square in the center of it. I used string and a laser level, just as if I were building a patio.

Now, not all quilters have laser levels, but they are a good thing. The one I have was inexpensive; I got it on Amazon for less than ten dollars. I had looked at the hardware stores around here, but they were too expensive, plus the salesmen didn't seem to want me to play with the lasers that much. The one I have shoots a horizontal line and a vertical line, both in red, along the wall. It has a level built into it and, thus, I am assured that my sixty-five-inch square is actually square. This thing will be amazing for hanging wallpaper.

While I was at the hardware store, I looked around for something that would work as a giant rotary ruler. It didn't have to have measurements marked on it; all I needed was a long, straight edge to either mark or cut along. I wanted four of them, so they had to be cheap. I found vertical blind panels in the window-treatment section. For fewer than ten dollars, I bought a package of a dozen. They are about eight feet long and a few inches wide. I think they may be light enough to pin onto my working wall when I need to mark the borders on this quilt. I don't want to try rotary cutting along a red line of light. I want a hard surface.

In order to get big pieces of fabric to dye, I buy rolls of prepared-for-dyeing fabric. I wanted to store them under the folding banquet table in my dye area. Those are the tables that have "H"-shaped legs. A big stick running through the cardboard tube of the fabric roll could rest on the horizontal part of the legs, like a giant paper-towel dispenser. Metal electrical conduit is the perfect thing to use for this. It comes in ten-foot lengths that are under two dollars. The only problem is getting a ten-foot pole into my car. I hadn't thought about this ahead of time, or I would have measured the table. I was at the hardware store looking for something else when I remembered I needed it.

Usually I go to the hardware store for some specific repair purpose and then spend an extra hour wandering around looking for stuff I can repurpose for quilting. The problem is that I don't have an encyclopedic knowledge of all the products out there, and the people who work in the big-box home improvement centers don't always seem to have the best imaginations. Very often, they just think I'm weird.

There used to be a retired dentist in downtown Grayslake whose family ran a small hardware store. He was fantastic. I could go in, describe what I wanted to do quiltwise, and he would come up with something. He introduced me to wooden drawer pulls screwed into strips of wood molding to make decorative quilt hangers. He sold me carpenter's squares to, well, square off the corners of my quilts. His other fine skill was to tell me what I needed to know ahead of time in order to do a repair. I could call him and tell him what problem my toilet was having—not running enough, running too much, etc.—and he'd tell me what to measure before I came in. Then he retired from being a retired dentist, and the store closed down.

Another hardware store opened up in town, and I had high hopes for it. One of the clerks was a retired construction guy. He was only working because his wife was getting tired of him hanging around the house. He helped me figure out how to use sawhorses to build a table out of three garage-door sections. He also helped me bend the knee-lift lever for my sewing machine, to make it fit better in my sewing cabinet. He finally fully retired too.

At the hardware store I realized that since banquet tables have "H"-shaped legs, I could hang a piece of pipe across the "H" and use that to hold up another roll of fabric. I thought I needed about six feet of pipe. I asked the clerk to cut it for me at the six-foot mark. I'd buy the whole ten feet in two pieces. We went to look for the guys who cut the pipe. The first two likely candidates insisted they don't cut pipe in the store, and I should buy a five-foot pipe. But I didn't want five feet, I wanted six. I went back to the pipe aisle. Brian had come along, and he was getting antsy. He hates the hardware store, because I tend to wander around and mention things we could be doing to the house. He does not like home repair. I'm sure I'd be annoyed if he took me to a kitchen store and pointed out all the good meals I could be making with the fancy pots and pans.

I prefer to go with a quilting friend. I have found that quilters, besides liking to go to quilt shops, have an affinity for office supply stores and home-improvement warehouses. Kathleen and I once ditched a jewelry class we took together to spend a few hours at a discount home-improvement store and came home with all kinds of tools and pieces of copper to make necklaces. Kathleen and I do not mention the home repairs we should be doing, and we most certainly do not ever discuss cooking.

Brian looked up and noticed the sign that said, "Pipe, cut to length." We went and got clerk number four to look at the sign. He pulled out his phone and called the store manager. She agreed that they do indeed cut pipe to length, just like the sign says. She told us to go to the plumbing department and find John. He was the pipe cutter. We headed for the plumbing department and found three more clerks, all standing around. (I think I forgot to mention the store had just opened that week, and there were more clerks than customers.) I asked for John, as he was the pipe-cutting clerk. A man who was not John suggested I could cut the pipe with a hacksaw. I replied, in a more polite tone than I felt at that point, that I didn't happen to bring a hacksaw along with me. (I declined to say that normally I *do* carry a hacksaw in my purse, but today, I left it at home.)

We then found John, who finally cut the pipe with a pipe cutter. (Which is a tool I *could* carry in my purse, but that would be weird.) I did own a pipe cutter, but I can't find it right now, which is really too bad, because the six-foot pipe should have been a five-foot pipe—it sticks out from under the table and is going to trip me. I need a five-foot pipe, and I think I know where to get one. If they don't have a five-foot pipe in stock, I'm going to buy a new pipe cutter and trim the pipe right there, proving that a pipe cutter is better than a hacksaw any day. And it fits in my purse.

When I Grow Up

Mary and I have been friends for about twenty years. The first time we met, that I remember, was at a machine-embroidery class given by dj Bennett in her home. The students were all squished together around her kitchen and dining-room tables.

Mary is older than I am—in fact, I'm closer to her daughter's age—but Mary is one of my closest friends. I can tell Mary just about anything. We share many common interests, and I admire her greatly.

A few years after my mother-in-law passed away, my father-in-law, Harold, came to visit for a few weeks. Harold and I were talking one day, and he told me that he'd begun dating again but was having a hard time with the independence of his lady friends.

"When I call them and invite them on a date, they say they have to check their calendar and get back to me. Shouldn't they be excited that I'm inviting them out and immediately accept?" he asked.

I explained to Harold that women in his age group, once widowed, were not simply waiting around for him to call them. They have other interests, and after raising families and taking care of husbands for so many years, they had other things to do with their time.

"For example," I said, "if you called my friend Mary in March and asked her out, she'd have to check the NCAA basketball playoff schedule to see if she was free. When the games are on, she stays home to watch."

"Really? What if I called and invited her to a game, in person? Would she go?"

I didn't know if she would, but it was an entertaining idea. Mary and my father-in-law shared a lot of common interests: sports, taking driving vacations. Mary likes to bring a lot of stuff with her when she drives, like a cooler to hold her coffee cream, so maybe she'd appreciate the little refrigerator Harold bought to plug into his van.

Harold passed away, so I never found out. I'm sure he would have appreciated Mary's television setup. She has a picture-in-picture TV next to a regular one, so she can watch three basketball games at once. She's our go-to woman whenever we have a sports question. I was wondering if Michael Jordan's son was playing at the college level yet. Mary told me who he plays for and his position, and she knew the team's record.

Mary and I email each other frequently; we live an hour away from each other, so this is how we stay close and in touch. We carry on long conversations via the computer—sometimes we even pick up the phone and call each other—and we like to have lunch together after guild meetings, or dinner beforehand, whichever works better in the schedule.

Mary is a total computer geek, and I admire her greatly for that. She's one of the few people I know who have a computer that runs Windows and actually understand how it works. Several years ago she switched over to the Mac operating system, so she changed her old PC to run Linux. I bet you don't even know what Linux is, unless you have your own resident computer geek.

Mary likes to have the latest technology, both computer-wise and in sewing. She was the first person I knew who got a dedicated embroidery machine. She's traded it in at least once for a bigger, better embroidery unit. Her serger can hold more spools of thread than anyone else's—she might be up to twelve spools for all I know.

Mary has always had a kind word to say about my quilting and has encouraged me every step along the way. She lends me equipment, like the light meter I needed to be able to take my own quilt photographs so I could send them to shows. I treasure her friendship, and I hope I am as cool as she is when I finally grow up.

An Old Friend with a Good Eye

Let me tell you about my friend Lynne Warner. We bonded our freshman year in high school, thirty-four years ago; we ate lunch together, and we still do that whenever we can. Lynne moved away from the Chicago area a few times, but now she's back, and this week we had a meal in our favorite haunt, Best Panda. Lynne and I are in many ways complete opposites: She's six feet tall, I'm under five feet. She's thin, I'm well-padded. Lynne is politically conservative and religiously devout, I'm at the opposite end. (Although I will say that in high school, I went along to the Young Life meetings, which were for Christians, but I went mostly because the boys were cute and I liked the music.) Lynne is very sweet, and I'm acidic and cynical. But, both of us have always sewn and enjoyed each other's company, and our friendship has stayed strong despite our differences.

We sewed our dresses for the school dances. In junior high, my home economics teacher didn't notice that I had an odd way of pinning the seams together. I would put pins, head to toe, along the entire seam and pull them out as I got to them. Lynne immediately noticed the folly and showed me how to put about *five* pins on each seam. If it weren't for her, I'd still be spending most of my time pinning. Unfortunately for her older brother, I learned how to sew things together without pinning at all, and there was this one time I sewed the pant legs shut on his favorite pair of blue jeans. He wasn't wearing them at the time.

Lynne's grandmother was a quilter, and a seamstress. She came to visit one year, and she and her daughter made fabulous drapes for their living room. I didn't know you could do that yourself! She also made quilts, and her Grandmother's Flower Garden was the first quilt I ever saw. Lynne then was spurred on to make a quilt for her boyfriend's graduation—very large half-square triangles from a pattern in the *Chicago Tribune*, back during the great quilt revival of 1976. I started quilting then too, but my first effort was a Drunkard's Path, in red, white, and blue. The pieces were cut with an electric scissors, and nothing fit together. The quilt parts have since disappeared, and I don't think that is something to be mourned.

I brought a boyfriend home from college one weekend, and Lynne said, "He's in love with you. I can tell by how he looks at you." That was Brian, and we are still married twenty-eight years later, so she has a good eye.

The Dangerous Quilter

My friend Kathleen is a dangerous quilter. She likes to use strong chemicals, and she has a lot of machines that could hurt somebody if not used properly. Luckily, she knows what she is doing and proceeds carefully. Kathleen has a doctorate in genetics and spent some time splitting frog eggs in half with knives made out of eyelashes. Thus, measuring dye powder and its associated chemicals is not a big deal to her.

Kathleen has been staying home while raising her children, and she has had time to explore many facets of the quilting world. She has discharge-dyed silk, using another dye to replace the color she removes; she has printed cloth using Jell-O; she has beaded on quilts; and, my favorite, she has used metal on the surface of art quilts.

Kathleen and I took a jewelry class together, and that started her exploration of equipment and chemicals, I think. She's very good at following a new direction in her work, and she's an expert at ordering new supplies over the Internet.

We will remove this page from the copy of the book I give Kathleen so she doesn't see the following list of her equipment:

1. Foredom Flex Shaft: This holds drill bits and other stuff to work metal. I think dentists also used to use these

on cavities. (Which makes me wonder if a lot of dentists also make jewelry; the two skills are not that different. My kid's dentist turned out to be an expert on porcelain artwork.) I shy away from this tool and have named it "The Spinny Thing."

2. Drill Press: Actually, I'm jealous of this one. It's a drill press that will put tiny holes in metal.

3. Bench shear: To cut pieces of metal in strips, or maybe to bend them. I'm not sure; the machine scares me. I don't have a nickname for it.

4. Metal roller: Another tool for metalworking. It lets you add texture to flat pieces of metal. I'm scared of this one too.

5. Torches: The torches we used in the jewelry class are crude compared to the ones living in Kathleen's basement. I'd love to try my hand at them, but I'm afraid I'd set her house on fire.

6. This thing that spins around and cleans off the edges and surfaces of metal. I'm totally afraid of this thing, as it can catch your work and toss it across the room, or into your face.

7. Two kilns. I can't remember why she has two, but she has them. I'm probably not afraid of those.

Essentially, Kathleen has all the equipment for a beautiful jewelry studio in her house, but I'm afraid of all of it, and she's grown bored with it. She moved on to knitting, and then to spinning, and now has a spinning wheel and a vast collection of fibers to spin—and even if she ran out of that, she has a good stash of knitting yarn.

Kathleen knits well, she makes beautiful jewelry, and she keeps very neat notes in her well-arranged notebooks, documenting all of her experiments.

While I don't do all the stuff she does, I do dye fabric. My careful measuring was laughable compared to hers, so I don't even bother. I just throw in a tablespoon of this, a half-cup of that. One day, we'll write a book together. The left side of each page can be Kathleen's detailed instructions; the right, my commentary on all of it, plus simplified directions that may not actually work that well.

Walter's Mother: An Old-Fashioned Quilter

My friend Walter had a mother who was a quilter. She lived near New Orleans and came to visit him for a while. She and I spent a day together, going to quilt shops in the area. When we came home, I showed her my quilts. Afterward, Walter told me that she was impressed with them but worried that I was working too hard on quilts that would never be valued, because I quilted them wrong. She was of the school that believed all quilting should be a quarter inch away from the seam, following the shape of each piece.

It's probably a good thing that I never showed her my rotary cutters and strip piecing. That would have probably upset her. That was even before I gave up piecing and started fusing my quilts together. I'm not sure at all what she would have made of them.

Walter's mother crocheted beautifully. After that visit, she sent me a cotton crocheted tablecloth. I set it aside, rarely using it, since we weren't formal diners. A few years later, we bought a queen-sized canopy bed, and I used the tablecloth as the canopy—it fits perfectly, held on by a few plastic tacks that many people use to baste their quilt sandwiches. Every once in a while, I clip the tacks, wash the tablecloth, and reinstall it. So far, it's lasted twenty years, and I see it first thing every morning. I wonder if Walter's mother, who passed away a while ago, would be happy knowing I use her handwork every day and that, eventually, my quilts found some acceptance. Even if I didn't quilt them the old-fashioned way.

Quilting Friends

True to my reputation as the Goddess of the Last Minute, I stayed up until two o'clock last night finishing a quilt, took photos this morning, and brought the film to the developer right when they opened. I need them back tomorrow. My quilt-show deadline is in four days.

I timed how long it took to get my quilt, lights, and camera set up to take the pictures. Fifty minutes.

Last week, my friend Kathleen was over, and we photographed her quilts. It took two hours, even working together. But that also included about an hour spent looking at her quilts, discussing her next quilt, looking at my quilt in progress, and deciding where to go for lunch—and, of course, clearing off my design wall, worktable, and floor (so nothing extra gets in the slides and I don't trip); and finding the film, the camera, the tripods, etc. Starting out with a cleaner workspace saved me an hour this morning.

If I hadn't helped Kathleen with her slides last week, I would have missed the pickup this morning on my own slides. There is no chance that I would have cleaned up my studio ahead of time. And Kathleen is taller than me, so she can clear off the top level of my working wall.

Which brings me to my point. Time spent with quilting friends is a good investment. Good friends are wonderful, but good quilting friends are even better. Although I prefer to make quilts in solitude, I know that no one would have ever seen any of them if I didn't have someone else to help me along the way.

Juried quilt shows need to see photographs of your quilt during the submission process. I had been taking my own slides but wasn't having much luck. A fellow quilter, Beth, decided to help me out, and that year, I got into the American Quilter's Society show for the first time. Beth and I still see each other on a regular basis, in a critique group that meets at her house.

I've helped other quilters take pictures of their own quilts, hoping a little help will give them a leg up too.

When I'm trimming thread, I use a scissors that hangs around my neck on a shoelace decorated with penguins and kiwi birds that my friend Helen Marshall sent me from New Zealand. Helen and I send stuff back and forth occasionally; in fact, our friendship started when I sent her some foil masking tape that she couldn't find in New Zealand. In 2002, Helen invited me to come visit her. Brian arranged the air travel, using his frequent flier miles. I suspect that Helen then realized I would be there for two weeks—a long time to host anyone—so she arranged teaching engagements for me all over the country. I didn't even see her until I'd been there for a full week.

At one point on that trip, I was taking the train from Greymouth to Christchurch. My fellow passengers included two couples on vacation, also from the United States. One of the husbands seemed to be in charge of their adventures. There was much discussion amongst them about hotels and transportation arrangements. He was a friendly man and soon brought me into the conversation, asking me the story of my trip. He wanted to know where I was staying in Christchurch.

"With Olive," I replied.

"Olive, is that a hotel?"

"No, Olive is a person. She's picking me up. I'll stay with her and teach a class for her quilting guild."

"What is Olive's last name?"

Not that it was his business, but I didn't have her last name on the tip of my tongue. It was on a note, with her phone number, buried in my purse somewhere. (I can almost always spot the quilter who meets me at the airport or train station.) He thought the whole thing was odd, but I made a bunch of new friends on the other side of the world, an adventure I would have never had without Helen.

During that trip to New Zealand, Helen set me up with Margaret Wickens, for a one-on-one felting class. Margaret makes felt the old-fashioned way, by laying out wool fibers, rolling them up in a bamboo window blind, and rolling, rolling, rolling the blind until the wool is felted. It's an arduous process. There are faster and easier ways to do it, but it was wonderful to learn the traditional method, and Margaret's work is amazing.

In January 2006, I got to go to Melbourne, Australia, to teach at the Australasian Quilt Convention. Since I would "be in the neighborhood," Helen suggested I stop by for a few days' visit in New Zealand.

We spent some time with Margaret. She had been knitting and felting and needed some needles that she couldn't find in New Zealand. I found them here in the U.S. and sent them "down" to her and, in the process, started knitting again myself.

Helen invited some of our mutual quilting friends over for dinner on that second trip. It was amazing to be sitting in a room full of friends from so far away. Betty and Jill had stayed at my house, along with Helen, when they were touring the U.S. Anne Scott and I see each other every once in a while when she visits the U.S. for quilt shows; she's the editor of *New Zealand Quilter* magazine.

We stopped in at Fibre Fair in Waikenae. I was perusing some quilt fabric with kiwi motifs when one of the clerks called out, "Robbi! A little bird told us you were in town!"

I think the little bird was Betty, but I have to tell you that the quilt shops in my hometown don't pay any attention to me most of the time, so it was pretty cool being welcomed to a quilt shop on the other side of the planet.

Quilting also brings opportunities to make friends out of strangers in the street. In Melbourne, the "real" purpose of the trip was giving the keynote presentation at their quilt show. Coincidently, that night there were fireworks downtown to celebrate Australia Day. When I left the convention center, I asked a man in a city-works uniform where the fireworks would be. He pointed down the river and asked why

I was in town. I told him about the quilt show, whereupon he whipped out his cell phone and showed me pictures of the quilt his "mum" made. He had one full view and several details of an art quilt his mother-in-law had created, and he proceeded to fill me in on how she did the lettering and what it stood for. I told him that any son-in-law carrying quilt pictures on his phone is a fine young man. And then two more quilters came along and we all watched the fireworks together, standing on a bridge over the Yarra River.

I taught for four full days in Melbourne. Wait, let me correct that. In Australia, they have morning tea, lunch, and then afternoon tea, so I taught in between the eating opportunities. Tea isn't just tea; tea can be coffee, and there are cookies and pastries. One afternoon, tea was ice cream bars. One convention delegate asked me if I thought it was odd to have ice cream for tea. Odd? No. Delightful? Yes. The best part about the afternoon tea was that we were all full of caffeine in the afternoon. My students stayed until dinnertime, working hard and finishing their projects. In the United States, sometimes we peter out at around three in the afternoon. At tea and lunch, I was adopted by "The Debbies": three women, obviously named Debbie—different spellings, but all from Perth, and all good friends. They'd save a place for me at the table, and when they noticed that sometimes I couldn't find the pastries or forks because I was last to leave the classroom, they started putting stuff on the table for me. Wasn't that nice?

I think I'm very lucky that my quilting takes me literally to the other end of the earth, and I treasure the friends I have made along the way, including visitors who have come to the U.S. from other countries for quilt shows. It's not just about the quilting, but the quilting gives us a common "thread," if you will.

Quilting friends are also wonderful to shop with. Lynne and I spent the afternoon at Linens 'n Things last week. We took one cart, piled it high, then edited at the checkout. I bought tablecloths to use in my living room on end tables and examined commercial comforters for the bedroom. I came home with a bunch of stuff and showed it to my husband, who just nodded while I went on and on about how beautiful this purple tablecloth was. Lynne was *way* more excited when I found it.

I went shopping with my husband last week, and he did not see the need to buy a coffeemaker, blender, stand mixer, and can opener in rainbow colors and arrange them on our kitchen counter. He pointed out that I don't cook anyway. Lynne, my best friend since my freshman year of high school, knows that I don't cook but would have urged me to buy the kitchen stuff, because she knows that colorful kitchen appliances are what inspired my series of fused quilts—and wouldn't they look great on my counter? Whether they get used is beside the point. The fact is, I've come to the conclusion that no matter how nice my kitchen looks, I'll never prefer to spend my time cooking when I could be making a quilt.

About the Author

Robbi Joy Eklow is a free-motion quilter and pattern designer who has been sewing since she was in kindergarten. For a while her love of science and math overcame her love of textiles, and she earned a degree in engineering from Purdue University. Robbi started her first quilt in 1976, during the Great Quilt Revival, and has been hooked ever since. Today she teaches and lectures internationally, and her distinctive, hand-dyed quilts have won ribbons in many major shows. Her quilt "Fantasy Flowers" is featured on the cover of this book; more of her quilts and sketches appear throughout.

Robbi writes the humorous column "The Goddess of the Last Minute" for *Quilting Arts Magazine* and is the author of *Free Expression: The Art and Confessions of a Contemporary Quilter*. She lives in Chicago, Illinois, with her husband and a studio full of thread and sewing machines. Her fabric lives in the bedroom closets that her children abandoned when they left for college.